60-MINUTE MENTORING

FOR LAWYERS AND LAW STUDENTS

SMALL COMMITMENTS, BIG RESULTS

IDEAS
INSTRUCTIONS
INSPIRATION

BY AMY TIMMER
AND MATTHEW CRISTIANO

ONE REALLY GOOD IDEA EVERY DAY
attorneyatwork @

Published by Attorney at Work, Lake Zurich, Illinois.
www.attorneyatwork.com

Illustrations © iStockPhoto.com

ISBN-13: 978-0-9895293-9-6

ONE REALLY GOOD IDEA EVERY DAY
attorney at **work** @®

DEDICATION

First and foremost, this book is dedicated to Lamarr and Smooth Jazz, the bus drivers Matt first approached to practice the concept of self-mentoring, and from whom he learned that the Universe really does listen, that anyone can mentor you, and that good things come from connecting with other people.

— Amy Timmer and Matthew Cristiano

ACKNOWLEDGMENTS

This book would never have been written were it not for the University of South Carolina Law School's Nelson Mullins Riley and Scarborough Center on Professionalism, and the National Legal Mentoring Consortium, both of which are dedicated to bringing together those of us interested in lawyer and law student professionalism and mentoring, so that we can be inspired to discover and do the things explained in this book.

The authors would also like to thank the people who read and critiqued the 2012 version of this book for us: Justice Douglas Lang of the Texas Court of Appeals; John Montgomery, then Director of the Nelson Mullins Riley and Scarborough Center on Professionalism; Lori Keating, then Attorney Services Counsel for the Lawyer to Lawyer Mentoring Program, Supreme Court of Ohio; Janet Welch, Executive Director of the State Bar of Michigan; Janene McIntyre, then President of the Lansing, Michigan Black Lawyers Association; Mary Chartier, then Board member of the Ingham County Bar Association, who directed the 60-Minute Mentoring Program with WMU Cooley Law School; and Yousef Farraj and Sharae Crosdale, then WMU Cooley Law School students.

The authors also thank Tim Johnson and Joan Feldman of Attorney at Work for their guidance and support.

ABOUT THE AUTHORS

AMY TIMMER is Associate Dean of Students and Professionalism at WMU Cooley Law School. She is a member of the full-time faculty and has taught Torts and Equity and Remedies for 21 years. She designed and oversees the implementation of Cooley's Professionalism Plan, which has earned the Gambrell Professionalism Award from the American Bar Association's Standing Committee on Professionalism. A key part of Cooley's Professionalism Plan involves mentoring for law students To that end, she established a 60-minute professionalism mentoring program with local bar associations, many aspects of which are featured in this book. She also helped design and participated in a study comparing traditional mentoring to episodic mentoring.

Dean Timmer is one of the founding members of the National Legal Mentoring Consortium, and currently serves as Executive Committee member and Chair of its Best Practices Committee. She presented at the 2010 and 2014 national conferences on legal mentoring and on episodic mentoring, and was a panel presenter on mentoring at the National Association for Law Placement 2012 conference. In addition, she has presented on law student professionalism and mentoring to law schools, attorney organizations, business groups, and at local, state-wide, and national conferences including the ABA, Association of American Law Schools, Higher Learning Commission, NALP Professionalism Consortium, Nelson Mullins Riley & Scarborough Center on Professionalism, National Institute for Teaching Ethics and Professionalism, Commission on Lawyer Assistance Programs, Council of Bar Admissions Administrators, National Conference of Bar Executives, National Conference of Bar Presidents, and the Association of Professional Responsibility Lawyers.

Previously, she worked in state government and practiced law in the litigation department of Honigman Miller Schwartz & Cohn.

Dean Timmer attributes any success she has ever achieved to the skills, attitude, knowledge, ethics, ideas, and inspiration shared with her by mentors, who are too numerous to name, but one in particular deserves mentioning: Don LeDuc, President and Dean of WMU Cooley Law School.

M

ATT CRISTIANO spent seven years working in the banking industry and two years as a missionary for his church before entering WMU Cooley Law School.

There are two mottos he and his family share: "You make time for the things you want to make time for" and "attitude is everything." These philosophies, along with advice and guidance from his wife and longtime mentor, Sandee, are the core values to which he attributes his professional success.

Since graduating from law school, Matt has had the opportunity to mentor college graduates as they enter the "real world" and continues to be mentored in his role as an Executive in Southern California by an executive coach and through networking. Mentoring always has been and will continue to be a huge part of his professional career.

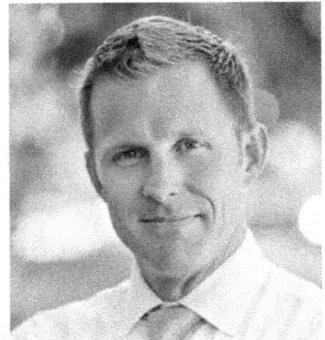

Matthew Cristiano

AUTHOR'S NOTE

The original version of this book was written when my co-author, Matt Cristiano, was a law student engaging in episodic mentoring at Western Michigan University Cooley Law School, and I was overseeing that program as Associate Dean of Students and Professionalism. In the past six years, Matt has gone on to be a successful attorney and continues to be struck by the value mentoring has brought to his life. Meantime, as I've traveled the country introducing the book through speeches and workshops, I've realized how greatly bar associations can benefit from creating episodic mentoring programs for their members.

In the past six years, more states have looked to mentoring to ease the introduction of new lawyers into the practice of law. At the same time, many affinity, local, and specialty bar associations have looked for ways to recruit and integrate new members into their existing membership using mentoring. The advantages are obvious: new attorneys need mentors not just to help them with legal issues, but to build a referral network, to become engaged with the legal community, to experience the values and customs of the local bar, to be exposed to continuing legal education and pro bono opportunities … and on and on.

There is no question that the legal profession continues to surge toward mentoring, especially to assimilate new attorneys into the profession.

So, we have added a new section dedicated to helping bar associations understand and utilize the concept of episodic mentoring. While much of the book is devoted to law students and new lawyers, and we have expanded information for mentors, it seemed natural to help bar associations help mentoring relationships flourish between those two groups — and to help them build and sustain bar membership.

We hope that this book will be useful to law students and lawyers seeking mentors and to those who would like to give back to the profession through mentoring. We hope it will be useful to bar associations seeking ways to provide meaningful mentoring without overburdening their resources, and to law schools seeking a way to offer mentoring to their law students — ideally, inspiring a desire to establish their own mentoring relationships with many more attorneys.

— Amy Timmer

CONTENTS

PART 1

FOR EVERYONE

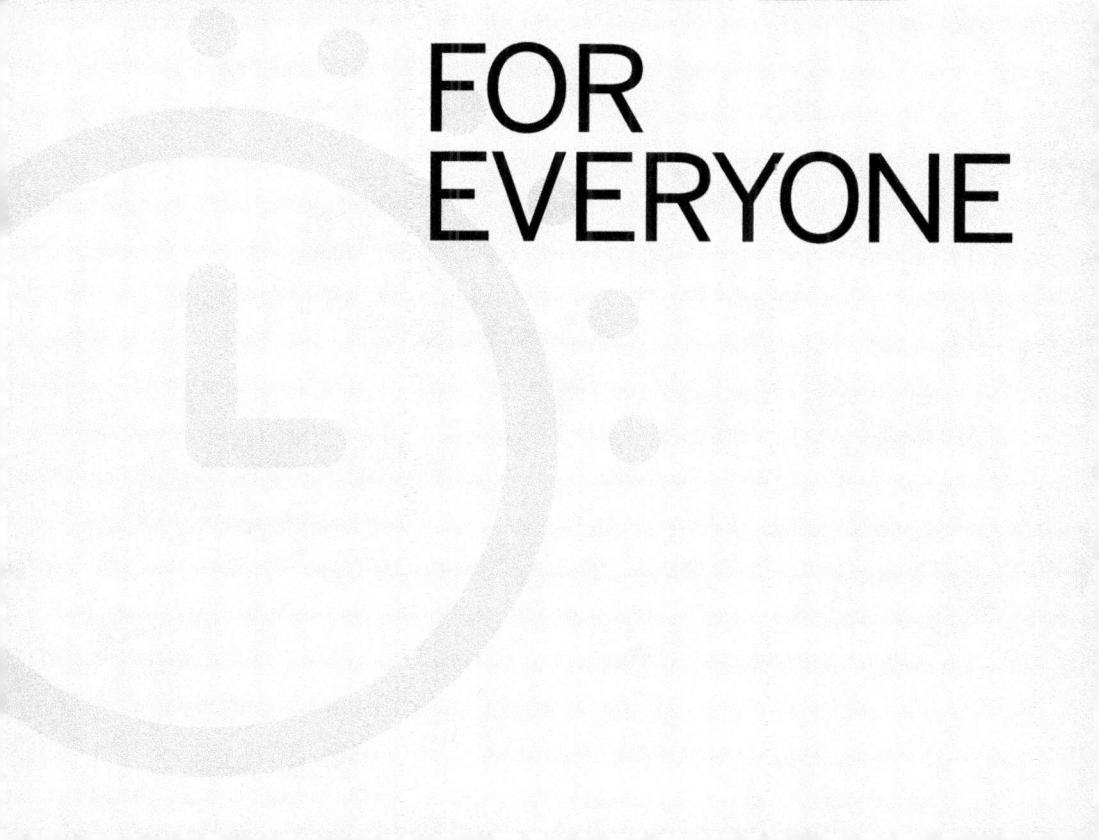

CHAPTER 1

WHAT IS MENTORING?
GUIDING AND CONSIDERING

Asking for Directions

Mentoring is teaching, advising, and guiding. Being mentored is learning, accepting, and considering. It's as simple as asking for and being given directions. It's just that the directions may be about the path to take in your life, and not just the turn to make up ahead.

MATT SAYS: When I started law school, I came with absolutely zero connections in the legal field, going to school 3,000 miles from home, in a state where I knew I would not stay after I graduated. I was not sure what I needed to do; I just knew that I needed to do something. During orientation, we had a presentation about a "professionalism class" that we could take. It was a low-commitment class that would encourage us to do a self-evaluation and prepare ourselves to be ethical and professional, but also teach us how to make connections in the legal field. One of the ways we did that was through mentoring.

We tend to believe, especially when we're younger, that we know it all and that what others have to offer is not valuable. Maybe you're thinking of a grandparent who wants to tell you about life before the internet or the days when folks could tune up their own car, and you really don't want to hear about it, especially not for the 100th time. The good news is we're not talking about opening yourself up to that kind of learning, although you will come to value such stories as you age.

We're talking instead about learning relevant skills, knowledge, and ideas that will help you in your career. Mentoring leads to being a better law student, lawyer, family member, and colleague. Mentoring will help you develop into a person who is proactive and in charge of your own life decisions, as opposed to one who constantly reacts to unexpected situations.

AMY SAYS: Younger people just starting out in a career make the mistake of thinking they shouldn't ask for help. It may be that they are embarrassed, or too proud, or overly confident, but I think more often they really believe they are somehow just supposed to know how to do whatever they've been hired to do. Well, you're not. Those of us who have lived longer and experienced more know with certainty that there are things mentors can help you with, about which you really need guidance.

Opening Yourself Up

If mentoring is about teaching and learning, then mentoring opportunities exist all around us, every day, with almost every human being we encounter. The trick, which we will repeat throughout this book, is to open yourself up to learning from others: Learn to accept rather than just give or react.

Don't think you have to be in the presence of supposed greatness to learn lessons that will help you in your life and career. If you pay attention and open your mind, you can learn from almost anyone in your vicinity. And the learning may be passive—like watching an angry customer get nowhere yelling at an overwhelmed store clerk or watching road rage turn into something deadly.

Personal Mentoring

Don't assume people in certain stations in life can't teach you something valuable. Parents are our first mentors because their mission is to teach us pretty much everything, starting with "that's hot and will burn you." But we are surrounded by others who are teachers if we let them be or ask them to be. Parents will tell you they learn from their infant children how to be better parents. Likewise, the person sitting next to you on the bus may have a nugget of wisdom to offer. Your spouse or significant other will become a lifelong teacher if you accept that they know more about some things than you do. Relationships thrive when partners acknowledge that each brings value, experience, and good ideas to the relationship. So on a very personal level, you might allow those closest to you to be mentors. They will help you become a better person.

Professional Mentoring

Professional mentoring can help with the challenges of a specific profession, such as transitioning from law student to lawyer or navigating the first years of law practice. But professional mentoring can also help you become a more professional person—it can help you *develop your professional identity.*[1] Professional mentoring is about growing in your role as a lawyer, or in your role as a law student preparing to be a professional.

Knowledge, Skills, and Ethics[2]

As a law student or new lawyer mentee, you will want to develop and exhibit characteristics of a successful professional, including your personal ethics, your work habits, your inquisitiveness, and your ability to get along with others. Here's a more complete list of the characteristics mentees can work on perfecting:

- Personal ethics including honesty and candor
- Dedication to thorough research and excellent work product
- Civility
- Inquisitiveness
- Patience
- Open-mindedness
- Dependability
- Preparation
- Cultural competence, including how to understand others
- Enjoying people

Likewise, you will want to build the skills you will require as a professional lawyer, including these 11, which are known as the MacCrate skills:[3]

1. Problem-solving
2. Legal analysis and reasoning
3. Legal research
4. Factual investigation
5. Communication
6. Counseling
7. Negotiation
8. Alternative dispute resolution
9. Litigation
10. Organization and management of legal work
11. Recognizing and resolving ethical dilemmas

MATT SAYS: When I first looked at the MacCrate skills, I more or less glanced at them. I thought to myself, no big deal, I am good on these; I only need to work on x or on y. The next time I looked at them, what an eye-opener! I did a little reality check. I needed development and help in every single category. In my opinion, I don't think you can ever truly master these skills; the things you need to work on multiply or become more complex.

You will also want to build these 10 additional skills:

1. Dealing with difficult people
2. Handling a budget
3. Running a meeting
4. Creating an agenda
5. Inspiring others to be their best
6. Strategic planning
7. Managing people, including focusing their work on a strategic plan
8. Billing clients
9. Marketing
10. Upholding the rules of professional conduct

Finally, you will need to acquire the knowledge necessary for the competent use of your law degree in your chosen area. You may have studied some of these topics in law school as electives. If not, you can pursue them through continuing legal education.

Now you know what it is you need to learn from others to develop professionally. So how will you go about finding people who can help teach you those things?

Networking to Create Episodic Mentoring Opportunities

If the word "networking" conjures up images of standing alone in a corner at a cocktail party, dreading every moment because you don't know a soul and don't really want to, put that right out of your head. Instead, think of networking as expanding the number of contacts you have who can help you in your career in any way.

Professional networking means meeting and maintaining relationships with professionals you can go to for help. You may never need their help, but they can become good colleagues if you keep yourself linked to them. In some cases, your network may comprise your closest colleagues. At other times, the link may be as tenuous as being connected on LinkedIn, the professional social networking site. Anyone who accepts your invitation to "connect" understands that you may be contacting them one day for assistance. And all of us have impliedly agreed to accept that contact.

But there will be times when you need someone to show you the ropes, write you a letter of recommendation, guide you to the resources you need, introduce you to someone you want or need to meet, and so on. That's what your network is for.

So it's as important to maintain your network as it is to develop one in the first place. Besides sending the dreaded "holiday letter," though, how do you develop a level of mutual understanding with people in your network? You "mentor" with them. You stay in touch with them. Mentoring brings quality to your network. Mentoring allows one professional to teach an important lesson to another professional. Mentoring strengthens relationships.

---

[1] William M. Sullivan, Anne Colby, Judith Welch Wegner, Lloyd Bond, and Lee S. Shulman, *Educating Lawyers: Preparation for the Profession of Law* (The Carnegie Foundation for the Advancement of Teaching, 2007), 129. "Professional identity is in essence, the individual's answer to questions such as Who am I as a member of this profession? What am I like, and what do I want to be like in my professional role? And what place do ethical-social values have in my core sense of professional identity?" Sullivan et al. at 135.

[2] We take this tag line from both the mission of our school, WMU Cooley Law School, and from Sullivan et al., the "Carnegie Report."

[3] Robert MacCrate wrote a comprehensive report for the American Bar Association in 1992 in which he laid out the skills one needs to function successfully as a lawyer. See "Legal Education and Professional Development: An Education Continuum," American Bar Association Section of Legal Education and Admissions to the Bar, 1992. The report has come to be known as the MacCrate Report and the skills as the MacCrate skills.

CHAPTER 2

TYPES OF MENTORING
SELF, TRADITIONAL MATCHED-PAIR, EPISODIC, REVERSE, ELECTRONIC, AND GROUP

We've come to think of mentoring as a particular type of professional relationship: one that is expected to endure for an extended period of time and is either based in or will hopefully promote trust between the two people involved, consisting of regular meetings between a professional (mentor) and a neophyte (mentee or protégé) that are supposed to be helpful to the protégé's professional development. Now that certainly is one type of mentoring, and you're lucky if you can find that.

But let's liberate ourselves from that model to consider a faster, easier, modern form of mentoring that allows you to have many mentors and is based on today's faster pace of life. First, let's understand how mentoring can occur.

Self-Mentoring

Law students and new lawyers have to be partners in their own development. Many people in your life can mentor you if you intentionally seek out what they have to offer. Even without their explicit approval or knowledge, you can gain information from them using your own techniques. This is called self-mentoring. Consider the following proactive self-mentoring techniques:

- Information seeking ("How do you know when to …?")
- Feedback seeking ("I am thinking about externing with the attorney general's office. What are your thoughts on that?")

- Relationship building ("I read about your pending case in the newspaper and would love to sit in on your upcoming trial.")
- General socializing ("How do you like being a member of this bar section?")
- Positive framing ("I have looked forward to meeting you because of your success in starting the professionalism orientation program at Michigan law schools.")
- Learning "language and customs" ("Your clerk was kind enough to explain to me when motion day is and how I can observe a trial in your courtroom.")[1]

Besides employing overt questioning, self-mentoring can occur through simple observation, as long as you train yourself to think about cause-and-effect as you watch something unfold. For example, watch how people handle difficult questions—questions they don't want to answer. Ask yourself how you might elicit the information you want by asking the question differently.

MATT SAYS: I love self-mentoring through observation. I used to call it "people watching." I would do it at places like Disneyland, downtown, or at the beach. In my Torts II class, our professor gave us an opportunity to argue a summary judgment motion where she would preside as the judge. When the day of the argument came, I thought I was prepared, but I did not feel comfortable. I went and watched three hours of arguments before mine. I felt so much more prepared after watching. My fellow students would not tell you that they were "mentoring" me, but I sure was learning from their mistakes.

You can also self-mentor through "disguised" conversations by asking a person to teach you without using that word. For example, start a sentence with: "Tell me about …" and then ask whatever burning questions you have. As you try this, be sure that you are "reading your audience." Start with questions that allow simple answers and work toward questions that may require a more in-depth response. You don't want to make the other person work at this conversation; you want to make it enjoyable for them. If they start to appear frustrated with your questioning, tone it down, tell a story, or change the subject.

The beauty of self-mentoring is that you control when and if it happens. Once you begin to use these techniques, you will find mentoring opportunities all around you. Just remember to open yourself up to learn from others.

Traditional Matched-Pair Mentoring

Most people reading this book probably know of this traditional approach. Two people pair off, one mentoring the other for an agreed-on, extended period of time. Often the pair agree to meet at certain intervals and cover certain topics that will be helpful to the protégé. When this works, it truly works, usually because the pair enjoys each other's company.

"Matched-pair" implies that someone else does the matching. Indeed, a mentoring study that we were involved in (which we'll discuss in more detail in coming chapters) used matched-pair mentoring for half of the study group based on a form the participants filled out expressing their wishes for a match. If both parties make a concerted effort, this type of mentoring can be remarkably successful.

Generally, matched-pair mentoring will occur when an institution decides to invest in the administrative structure required to recruit the participants, train them, make the matches, suggest the agenda, monitor the relationships, and address issues that arise. If you have a chance to engage in a matched-pair mentoring program, try it out. The one element that may ensure the match's success is that participants on both sides are interested and willing to commit to the effort.

At law firms, new associates are often assigned mentors. They tend to be the person the young associate can go to with questions that they may hesitate to ask other lawyers. Law firms report varying success with these programs (probably based on personalities that click or don't). If you give it serious thought, you can see the potential pitfalls of an assigned mentoring relationship. What if the two don't get along? What if the senior attorney expresses a romantic interest in the protégé, or vice versa? What about the uneven power base of the two people involved? These are not uncommon issues in the workplace, and they become more difficult when the new lawyer is directed to have a working "mentoring" relationship with the senior attorney. However, many firms have set up mentoring programs that address these issues, and they work well. Whether and how a given firm offers mentoring is something any lawyer seeking a job there should consider and explore during the interview process.

Episodic, or 60-Minute, Mentoring

Throughout this book, we promote the concept of episodic mentoring, and we offer specific instruction on how lawyers, law students, and bar associations can implement it in place of a traditional matched-pair mentoring program. Simply put, **episodic mentoring is based on short-term episodes between two people focused on a particular topic.** The episodes may be as short as 20 minutes or as long as a couple of hours, but one hour seems to be the most popular time increment, thus the moniker "60-minute mentoring." The purpose is to engage in focused mentoring during a short time span, to allow the mentor and mentee to explore one topic.

A mentoring episode can be created solely by the two people who engage in it. Generally, a protégé may reach out to a seasoned attorney to ask for some time to explore a concern. But seasoned attorneys are encouraged to reach out to law students or new lawyers, especially those in their own firm, bar association, or local law school. The episodes can also be arranged by a law firm, bar association, or law school, but then the only matching should be by availability. Any attorney can engage any mentee in episodic professionalism mentoring. The point really is that exposure to diverse opinions and ideas is better for a mentee than one way of thinking that may be espoused by a long-term mentor.

These kinds of helping sessions between seasoned and new attorneys are nothing new. But episodic mentoring is an intentional focus on short-term episodes because, often, **much more can be gained through focused, short-term mentoring than through casual conversations,** which are sometimes what long-term mentoring relationships devolve into.

Even better, episodic mentoring can bring focus to topics often overlooked. This book is geared toward using professionalism and ethics as a first-time and often repeated topic of mentoring episodes. Legal communities are struggling with how to maintain or promote professionalism, civility, and camaraderie among their members. Trying to do that through a traditional matched-pair mentoring program may be hit-or-miss because the mentoring relationship may never address these issues specifically or directly. In comparison, episodic professionalism mentoring requires the mentor and mentee to talk for a half-hour or an hour about professionalism. The seasoned attorney will have much to say on this topic and the mentee needs to understand the emphasis on professionalism in the mentee's new circle of acquaintances.

Episodic mentoring is becoming more popular as a way to address the problems discovered when associations, firms, or law schools have failed at establishing lasting traditional matched-pair mentoring programs. Those traditional programs are fraught with challenges that range from the intense administrative work and resources required to identify, match, train, monitor, and re-pair the matched pairs, to the unhappiness a pair may experience when there is a bad match or a match simply fails to occur. Further, lawyers may not be interested in being matched for up to a year with someone they don't know, and mentees may be alarmed at the idea that they can have only one mentor.

AMY SAYS: When a young person approaches me and wants to learn from me or about me, I am flattered and receptive. I generally remember that person and usually have a positive feeling about them. It's a natural reaction to being asked about oneself. So protégés, keep in mind that being mentored (asking questions) can lead to a lasting relationship.

And as it turns out, these mentoring episodes can accomplish so much more than problem-solving—they can be the start of a relationship that can grow into one of trust and openness, and the end result can be a naturally occurring long-term mentoring relationship. In addition, mentees can have mentoring episodes with many lawyers and not feel restricted to just one mentor. That helps them get to know more attorneys, expand their network, and, most important, get many different viewpoints on one topic.

In this book, we mean to spread the word about the benefits of episodic mentoring, especially for law students and new lawyers, as well as for bar associations and law schools attempting to establish mentoring programs. Chapter 3 explores the benefits in depth, while later chapters are dedicated to bar association and law school mentoring programs.

Reverse Mentoring

Even seasoned attorneys who view themselves as all-knowing teachers can learn much from younger people. Let's start with the technology gap and end with a better understanding of the younger generation, and consider everything in between. The protégé can teach the mentor. The student can teach the teacher. Any good teacher knows that.

Reverse mentoring is nothing more than changing positions so that the protégé is guiding the mentor. Not only is it unexpectedly fun, it's a compliment to the other person. It may not be so simple, though, if the seasoned attorney is uncomfortable switching positions. The seasoned attorney may have to deliberately prepare for such a session, thinking in advance about what can be learned from the mentee. That may require opening one's mind to what the mentee has to offer. Don't worry—there are tips on that in the section for mentors.

Electronic, or by Email, Mentoring

While mentoring can occur by email, it probably shouldn't continue in that format beyond a couple of exchanges, simply because email is not as conducive to the kind of give-and-take that occurs during an in-person mentoring episode. More-senior mentors may not be as adept at typing, and will likely prefer conversation to email. Still, mentoring can occur by email when necessary. (On a related note, in our previously mentioned mentoring study, one student sought to be mentored through Twitter, asking famous attorneys throughout the country for their best career advice in 140 characters.)

But do consider using email forums, which provide a really great form of mentoring through group email discussions. You may find forum discussions going on about legal issues, judges, and pending cases that are newsworthy. By joining in those discussions you can learn a lot about how lawyers perceive current events and issues. Many lawyer organizations (that a law student can join, like a county bar association) offer these forums.

At Western Michigan University Cooley Law School, we often urge our students to review our alumni database—which lists alumni by both practice and geographic areas—to identify attorneys who are in the practice or place that the student is interested in, and to reach out to them by email. I usually suggest that students use email just to make the initial contact to arrange a time to talk by phone or in person, although some report that they engage in mentoring "conversations" with the attorney via email. If the mentor proposes that or makes it clear they are comfortable with it, then you could try it. But many people are not fans of offering advice by email.

Group Mentoring

At our law school, we organized a 60-minute mentoring program that schedules times when willing attorneys will meet for one hour with law students. We've found some benefit in sending groups of three to four students to meet with one attorney when the attorney prefers that. This generally happens when attorneys plan to share certain ideas they believe any student will benefit from (like ethics and professionalism concepts), as opposed to an open-ended give-and-take with just one person. If the attorney agrees, it makes sense to have a group of protégés all benefit from the same presentation, rather than the attorney repeating the information on four different occasions to single listeners.

Many attorneys and judges would enjoy and prefer the ease of a group conversation. Certainly, protégés who are shy might also prefer to meet with an attorney with two or three other protégés present. (See Chapter 7.) Note that some state mentoring programs provide group mentoring to new attorneys, particularly those who are unemployed and don't have a work setting in which to seek mentoring.

We have found some limited value in triangulated mentoring, which involves a law student, a new attorney, and a seasoned attorney. The idea is for the three of them to teach and learn from one another. But this requires a balance of personalities so that two of the three people don't dominate the conversation.

Summary

Mentoring, like teaching, can occur in a number of different forums and styles. You may want to experience all of them to decide what you prefer. You may find that each style has value and that you can be mentored or serve as a mentor in many different ways to accomplish different goals.

---

[1] See Kathy E. Kram and Belle Rose Ragins, *The Handbook of Mentoring at Work: Theory, Research, and Practice* (Sage Publications, 2007).

CHAPTER 3

UNDERSTANDING EPISODIC MENTORING
LESS COMPLICATED, MORE EFFICIENT, AND MUCH MORE ENJOYABLE

From the Business World to the Legal Field

Author Amy Timmer discovered episodic mentoring at the Nelson Mullins Riley and Scarborough Center on Professionalism's mentoring conference in 2007, where Dr. Kathy Kram[1] spoke about it based on her studies of such mentoring in business. Amy was searching for a way to offer mentoring programs at Cooley Law School, without many resources and across Cooley's campuses. Although Dr. Kram didn't emphasize this, what came through in her presentation was that episodic mentoring could be accomplished without a lot of administrative effort and could contribute to a person's growth and confidence in ways that being mentored by just one person could not. That became the model for episodic professionalism mentoring at Cooley and in this book.

Traditional versus Episodic Mentoring

Millennials (born between roughly 1984 and 2004) comprise much of the newest generation of attorneys. Those of us who are not millennials think of this new generation as one that moves quickly—sometimes too quickly. Everything in the lives of millennials, including written communication, information dissemination, shopping, downloading, researching, dating, and speaking, is set up to happen quickly and simultaneously. The older generations tend to think that faster is probably not better. We might be missing the boat—even the slow boat.

Could faster be better? It can be, especially in one area where traditional ways of doing things really do slow down a process unnecessarily.

Think of traditional mentoring. To set up a mentoring relationship the old-fashioned way, first you have to recruit people who want to be mentors and people who want to be mentored. Then you must collect enough information from those people to have some idea of how you might match those desiring mentoring with those desiring to mentor. There may be training involved. Then you have to introduce the parties to each other. You also have to give them either a list of activities they could engage in or meetings they could have with one another during which, it is hoped, the mentor might share a bit of wisdom with the mentee.

Typically, mentors are asked to take their mentees to lunch once a month. Or to bring them along to meetings and events, or introduce them around. Or to invite them to shadow the mentor. Or to exchange emails regularly. You get the idea.

Then someone, probably the same person who set up the match in the first place, has to monitor the pair to see if they are meeting and talking. Both mentor and mentee may have to report back to this administrator. After about a year, the administrator may check in with the pair to see how it's going: "Oh, you're not getting along? Not meeting regularly? Well, let me set you up with someone else then," and the process begins anew.

It may have taken a year for all that to happen, only to end up back at square one, perhaps with two people who are forever soured on the concept of mentoring. When a bad match occurs or trouble arises in the relationship, those involved may leave the experience swearing, "I'll never do that again!"

60-Minute Mentoring: Make It Snappy

Now imagine a faster, less complicated system. Two people get together for one hour and talk about professionalism. That's it. That's the whole thing: 60-minute mentoring.

The more experienced person likely has useful thoughts on professionalism. The less experienced person likely has questions or things on their mind about their own professional development. They talk together about those things.

No one has to match these people, other than by their mutual availability. When it's over, there needn't be follow-up (although there can be). The pair is not required to try to maintain a long-term commitment (although such a relationship may naturally develop). That is especially nice when the two may have nothing in common other than the conversation they just engaged in. No follow-up is required, no monitoring or evaluation.

When two people come together for this very defined purpose, odds are they will share something of value with each other. In fact, the chances of a valuable exchange might be better in these circumstances than in a forced relationship. Each person—but especially the mentee—will come away from the mentoring episode somewhat transformed in that they will have acquired from the brief encounter a deeper and broader understanding of something very important (professionally and personally).

Even Briefer Encounters

Now think of even briefer encounters. Imagine picking someone's brain in the elevator. One student struck up a conversation with a judge while they were both waiting for the elevator by saying, "Good morning, Judge," and then asking whether she would be on the bench that day hearing cases. When the elevator arrived, the judge was telling the student about a particular motion she was looking forward to hearing that day because it involved an interesting area of the law. By the time the elevator doors opened again, the student had been invited to sit in and observe motion day. The student did indeed stop into that court at the appointed time. The judge noticed the student's presence, and asked him to stay after the hearing ended. She then introduced the student to the lawyers on each side of the case and the student and lawyers stayed in the courtroom for a half-hour discussing what had just occurred. That student now had an opportunity to stay in touch with both the judge and the lawyers, adding three lawyers to his network. He was tremendously excited about what he learned that day.

What Episodic Mentoring Isn't

Episodic mentoring may be attractive initially because of its simplicity. It does not require recruiting or matching attorneys and protégés. It doesn't require a commitment from either party of more than an hour. It doesn't involve having to dream up events to attend together or working at finding regular times to meet. It is not a free-flowing conversation but is focused on one topic, initially ethics and professionalism. If the two people involved don't really click or get along, they never have to meet again. No one has to intervene to fix the relationship. There is no training involved for either party, and no evaluation at the end (although there can be both).

Because it is none of these things, episodic mentoring is more affordable as no resources have to be dedicated to administering a program, less intimidating because the pair never have to see each other again, and more productive because there is an assigned topic with limited time to cover it. But there are qualitative advantages to episodic mentoring, too.

Confidence-Building and Engagement through Episodic Mentoring

As we engaged in episodic mentoring at Cooley Law School, benefits we had not originally anticipated started to emerge.

For one, students became more confident. Some came out of their shells and found that they could not only approach attorneys they didn't know for help, they could also enjoy the time they spent together and come away with an entirely different outlook. Once you understand how to ask for and receive guidance, you find you can do it anywhere with anyone. Mentees who become comfortable with the concept of episodic mentoring feel freer to reach out to more and more attorneys. They may use the advanced search on Martindale.com to find attorneys from their law school, hometown, practice area, specialty, or combinations of those. They may send tweets to famous attorneys to seek their best snippets of advice. They may be more likely to join the local and state bar association because they have experienced firsthand the benefits of networking. They may come to love engaging with others, for the sheer pleasure of expanding their relationship base or tackling issues and improving the profession.

Best of all, they may be more likely to become mentors themselves.

Episodic Mentoring and Diversity

Mentees also learned that different attorneys have different opinions because they have had different experiences, all of which can be helpful for a budding attorney to learn about. And indirectly, they learned not to assume that what one person thinks is right or wrong; rather, it's just one person's perspective.

Before the concept of "diversity" became widespread, mentoring was stuck in molding people in the likeness of the mentor. What is most revolutionary to older attorneys, and may be simply obvious to younger people, is that that concept of mentoring has been flipped on its head. We have figured out that a diversity of opinion and life experience is what enriches us the most in our own growth. Mentoring with many different people allows us to share experiences that others have had that have shaped their outlook. And perhaps that will shape our own. At a minimum, the more ideas and opinions to which mentees are exposed, the broader their thinking.

When it comes to ethics and professionalism, that breadth is essential. Protégés need to understand that no one person has all the answers, and that the protégé's professional obligation may be to search out many ideas before concluding what is right or wrong, regulated and not, required or optional. (The next chapter explores the diversity question in more depth.)

Could This Be the Start of Something Lasting?

If you get the chance to engage a lawyer in a mentoring episode during which you learn something, consider whether that contact might actually evolve into a mentoring relationship, or even just another meeting. The relationship is not necessary, but it would be a wonderful addition to your continuing professional development. Long-term mentoring relationships last because they are based on mutual trust. A mentoring episode gives both parties the chance to explore whether a trusting relationship might evolve with continuing meetings.

Lifelong Mentors

A lifelong mentor is typically someone older or with more experience than you. Imagine someone who can teach you, take you under his or her wing, someone you can make mistakes in front of, someone you look up to. This person does not have to be in the same field as you. It can just be someone who listens and offers advice. Look around for family friends, work acquaintances, even business acquaintances who may be in a different line of work but with whom you are comfortable.

A mentor can also be someone who is near your age or even younger, and can be someone who does not have the same experience you have. It may be a classmate or a buddy from the gym.

If we are lucky, sometime in our careers we do connect with one person whom we trust and admire, and may even want to emulate. Such relationships are among the most valuable we will ever experience. If this person is your boss, count yourself among the luckiest of employees. If you are in the working world and haven't yet experienced this, look around at your superiors (in age, experience, or employment level) and try some self-mentoring techniques with them to see what might develop.

Don't overthink this. When you are looking for someone to trust completely, someone you can tell even the embarrassing truths to, the one person you can go to when you are afraid to go to anyone else, open your mind to the possibilities. This person could be your childhood friend or spouse, a colleague, boss, or employee.

The Study

The impetus for this book came from co-author Matt Cristiano, who had volunteered to participate in a study at the law school comparing episodic to traditional mentoring. Matt ended up being randomly selected to participate in the episodic mentoring group. That meant he was not assigned a mentor and had to go out into the world and find attorneys who were willing to mentor him for an hour. Being an introvert, that was overwhelming for him. But he did it and it changed his life, as it did for so many of the law students featured in Chapter 9 (which discusses feedback on the study). He suggested to Amy that they write this book from the dual perspective of mentor program administrator and law student mentee.

After the mentoring study was completed, Amy and three co-authors published an article about it in Australia's *Legal Education Review*.[2] The study found episodic mentoring to be a valuable type of mentoring that assisted law students in their professional development. In some ways, it was found to be more helpful than traditional matched-pair mentoring, particularly in providing to mentees many opinions and varying guidance, rather than only one person's guidance.

Creating Learning Moments

Call it speed mentoring. Call it episodic mentoring or 60-minute mentoring. Just keep this in mind: When you learned something that changed your life, something that really left an impression on you, something that you decided to incorporate into your being, did it take a year with someone to get that nugget? Or did you hear one line in a speech that touched you; get one bit of advice from a colleague that changed everything; overhear something interesting on a bus that resonated with you; read one sentence in a book that made you put down the book for a moment and mull it over? (Cue: Put down this book right now and mull.)

Momentous things can happen in a moment and episodic mentoring creates such moments.

---

[1] See Kathy E. Kram and Belle Rose Ragins, *The Handbook of Mentoring at Work: Theory, Research, and Practice* (Sage Publications, 2007).

[2] Eileen S. Johnson, Amy Timmer, Dawn E. Chandler, & Charles R. Toy, "Matched vs. Episodic Mentoring: An Exploration of the Processes and Outcomes for Law School Students Engaged in Professional Mentoring," *Legal Education Review* Vol. 23, No. 1 (Fall 2013).

CHAPTER 4

PERSPECTIVES ON DIVERSITY IN EPISODIC MENTORING

SHOULD WE BE LIKE, OR UNLIKE, ONE ANOTHER?

Promoting Sameness: It Depends

Whether to mold the protégé in the likeness of the mentor depends on what you are trying to accomplish. A group considering a traditional matched-pair mentoring program may have a goal of inculcating new members with the thinking and values of current members. For example, political organizations, religious groups, and advocates for certain underrepresented communities may want to promote a shared value system, work ethic, and even worldview. If that is the goal, it must be intentionally stated and members will likely require some training or guidance in how best to pass along those stated values and views to their protégés. Also, it may be important to pay attention to matching mentors and mentees by gender, gender identity, race, ethnicity, age, practice area, or other factors important to the organization.

Some organizations may not be promoting sameness in the qualities of their members, but may nevertheless find it important to match by gender or gender identity, race, age, or ethnicity. Certainly, matching by race, age, gender, or ethnicity may bring comfort to the new member who would then have the opportunity to see one of their own as a successful role model in the organization. On the other hand, some organizations find that, to promote diversity and inclusion, it is important to create mentor-mentee relationships between different races, ages, and genders.

Matching by gender or gender identity might avoid inappropriate sexual advances, which can plague traditional matched-pair mentoring, especially if it is based in unequal levels of power (partners with new associates, for example). Relative power within the organization and supervisory responsibilities should be considered. Matching by age or experience—for example, pairing new members with mentors who have been there only about a year—may be desirable to accomplish certain goals, but could be impossible or impractical depending on the age and experience of the new members, as well as the number of mentees. Pairing by age or experience is the traditional basis for mentoring (matching the more experienced with the less experienced), but it need not be.

The point is to recognize that while traditional matched-pair mentoring may be important to accomplishing certain inculcation goals, it may create problems that the program administrator did not anticipate and that are difficult to avoid when dealing with a limited pool of people, as in a law firm or local bar association. But it is equally important to see that a version of episodic mentoring—using a pool of mentors who are all available for 60-minute chats, but all of whom also share a characteristic important to the mentoring program—may improve the chances that the mentee will still reap the benefit of many mentors while focusing on a common value of the group.

No Matching Required

The concerns just discussed are endemic to traditional matched-pair mentoring, and so they may be irrelevant in pure episodic mentoring programs. An organization considering employing episodic mentoring will quickly realize that the goal is for each protégé to meet with as many members (or others outside that organization) as possible. Because no long-term match exists, problems that may crop up in one episode can be avoided by having no further episodes between that pair.

A key advantage, and inevitable outcome, of episodic mentoring is diversity of thought, ideas, and guidance because the mentee will have many mentors. Racial, ethnic, age, gender, and gender identification matches will be coincidental, if they occur at all. And protégés can seek out their own mentors, so if they desire to be mentored by someone like them—in whatever aspect—they can seek out that trait in the attorneys they decide to approach.

More-seasoned attorneys may think none of this really matters—that mentoring is mentoring, regardless of such traits. But people charged with creating and administering a mentoring program are often plagued with these concerns, so episodic mentoring can bring real relief to them by leaving these concerns in the hands of the mentee seeking mentors.

A word of caution, though, to those who decide to seek mentors who they think are like them in some way: Keep your mind open, as you may quickly learn that people you think are similar to you in some obvious way may not be similar at all in their approach to the world.

Is Any Structure Required in Episodic Mentoring?

You may be starting to see that various goals may prompt various mentoring structures. Even using episodic mentoring, a program administrator can still impose some structure, primarily by directing the mentees to only certain members of the group as mentors. So, for example, mentees may mentor with just the lawyers in their practice area, both inside and outside the organization. Or a Young Lawyers Section of a bar association may mentor exclusively with the Senior Lawyers Section. Law students may be directed to mentor with just alumni of that law school.

Further, if new members are obviously different from the current membership, like new minority female associates in a predominantly white male law firm, the program administrator should pay special attention to ensuring equal access to mentors and to coaching both the mentee and mentor to openly address these concerns.

Those who decide to open the pool of possible mentors to *any attorney* must be prepared to help the mentee identify and meet attorneys, research their discipline history, and be ready with questions and goals for the session so the attorney's time will not be wasted and the session is as productive as possible. Later chapters offer specific guidance on all these issues.

CHAPTER 5

THE FOCUS ON ETHICS AND PROFESSIONALISM: THE COMMON BOND
WHAT IS PROFESSIONALISM?

What is "art"? What is "obscenity"? You know it when you see it.[1] Perhaps the same can be said for "professionalism," but many excellent references discuss what we mean in the legal profession when we say this word. Readers can turn to the so-called "Carnegie Report" on educating lawyers,[2] and to resources like those listed at the end of this book.

What many lawyers seem to mean today by "professionalism" is civility—respecting others and their opinions and maintaining decorum. But "professionalism" also means adherence not just to the rules of professional conduct but also to values of right and wrong, dedication to continual self-improvement (including through mentoring), giving back to the community, providing access to justice, taking responsibility for one's actions, being prepared, putting the client first, recognizing conflicts, understanding cause and effect when it comes to one's behavior—and those are just some of the professionalism characteristics. You see, that opens up a lot of room for discussion during a mentoring episode, which may very well start with a conversation about what professionalism means in that particular legal community or in general.

Why Professionalism Matters

Mentoring programs exist, in part, to enculturate new lawyers and teach them the ways and values of the local bar and bench, to help them in their practice of law, to bring the legal community closer in its shared values, and to perpetuate access to justice. Many lawyers today are especially concerned about the lack of civility and preparation they witness in new attorneys. **Mentoring provides a way to bring along the next generation in sharing the values and practices established by those with years of experience.**

Further, the legal profession is facing disruptions caused by rapidly changing practices, technology, generational differences in values and behavior, costs, and public perception. As we navigate our way through these changes, we need a way to work with the next generations of lawyers, to take advantage of the skills and perceptions they bring to the table. Professionalism mentoring brings seasoned lawyers together with inexperienced lawyers and gives them the professional foundation from which to face these disruptive challenges successfully.

And most important, these conversations may make an immediate impact in helping the protégé avoid mistakes that can lead to malpractice or grievance claims.

On the Disciplinary History of Mentors

It may seem counterintuitive to send a protégé for professionalism mentoring to an attorney who has been disciplined. But an attorney who has been disciplined may make an outstanding episodic mentor, especially in the area of professionalism. That attorney has experienced—in a very personal way—the rules of professional conduct and the importance of adherence to the ethics rules. Such attorneys who have reformed their conduct and their viewpoint to strictly adhere to ethical conduct can pass along to a mentee the extremely valuable lessons they have learned from their experience.

Of course, there may be unrepentant disciplined attorneys who have not reformed their conduct, who have become bitter, who continue to labor under an addiction without seeking help, or who are somehow misguided in their thinking and approach to practice. They obviously should not be mentoring new attorneys or law students. How would protégés know which type of disciplined attorney they are researching? They won't, unless another person with personal knowledge of the situation can tell them with absolute certainty. Hence, protégés must keep their eyes wide open as to the type of attorney they are seeking advice from.

The way we see it, you can never know for sure who you are mentoring with, whether in a traditional matched-pair mentoring program or an episodic program. There may be an unethical practicing attorney who has not been caught (yet) and who volunteers to be a mentor. (Notice the similarity between episodic mentoring and dating? The same advice applies: Do your research but realize that you still don't know for sure who you are meeting up with.) You might have volunteer attorney-mentors who follow the rules of professional conduct but who are jerks.

And you might have disciplined attorneys who are now among the most ethical and respected attorneys around. What a program administrator can do is warn the mentees to do their research, pay attention, and decide whether they should continue to mentor with that attorney.

It's important for mentees to research the disciplinary history of a potential mentor for a number of reasons:

- They learn if such a history exists and where to find information on it. Part of an episodic mentoring program should focus on pointing mentees to specific resources they will need for their research.

- They learn the importance of researching other attorneys to find out more about their future partner, referral resource, colleague, or opponent—not just their discipline history but their reputation, past cases, community involvement, position in their firm, practice areas, and so on.

- They learn the importance of being educated about judges in front of whom they will appear

- Finally, as mom always said, "You need to know who you're talking to." In this day and age when research resources are always at our fingertips, there is no reason not to use them.

Professionalism as a Mentoring Topic

Professionalism is a broad enough topic that any lawyer can ask about it or talk about it. (See the "Template for Professionalism Mentoring" in Chapter 14, in the section for mentors.) But beyond that, professionalism is the perfect foundation from which to begin mentoring because it is essential to our profession. And with episodic professionalism mentoring, the program administrator need not be concerned with matching the parties by practice area or background. In the Quick References section at the end of this book, mentees will find questions they can ask mentors related to professionalism, and in later chapters, bar associations can find specific programming ideas and questions to use in various formats.

---

[1] "I know it when I see it" is a phrase made famous by U.S. Supreme Court Justice Potter Stewart, who used it in 1964 to describe his threshold test for obscenity in *Jacobellis v. Ohio.*

[2] Sullivan et al., *Educating Lawyers: Preparation for the Profession of Law.*

PART 2

FOR
MENTEES

CHAPTER 6

FIND, PLAN FOR, AND MAXIMIZE MENTORING EPISODES

WHY TO DO THIS, HOW TO MAKE CONTACT, WHAT TO ASK

What Mentors Can Do for You: The Protégé's Perspective

If you are reading this book, you must already believe that mentoring can help you, or you have at least heard of it and want to learn more. As a potential fan of mentoring, think about these possible ways a mentor could assist you:

- Help you with specific concerns about law school or lawyering.
- Expose you to the legal world through shadowing and discussion.
- Supervise you in his or her pro bono work or join you for public service work.
- Discuss legal issues that you need help with and share knowledge about areas of law.
- Educate you about a specific practice area.
- Describe how he or she balances work and personal life.
- Share professional experiences and insights that will help you grow.
- Be a role model for appropriate, professional behavior and teach you about professional conduct and development.

- Talk with you about your own professional development plan and review your professionalism portfolio.
- Introduce you to people who employ their law degrees in ways that interest you and help you develop a network of attorney contacts.
- Teach you about ethics challenges and how to handle them.
- Review your résumé and cover letter and write a letter of recommendation.
- Conduct a mock interview with you.
- Introduce you to people who are looking for externs or employees.
- Give advice on how to make a successful transition from law student to bar examinee to attorney, and the good moves and mistakes he or she may have made in the process.
- Attend professional events with you, such as bar association meetings.
- Allow you to do some legal research or writing.

With episodic mentoring, you may have many mentors to help you with various items on this list—without overburdening one person. Plus, in our experience, episodic mentoring leaves a much more positive impression and is less stressful for both mentor and protégé.

Think of mentoring like learning another language or about another culture. You can teach yourself through watching people or studying books, but it is not until you immerse yourself in it that you will realize all the benefits that come with being a protégé.

MATT SAYS: I am not sure if I have learned more about other attorneys and being a lawyer, or more about myself through my mentoring experience. You see, in my opinion, mentoring is not something that is ever completed. Anyone who wants to move forward in life, move up in a career, or end up in a leadership position will always be looking for advice on how to become better at their position, or move up even higher, and they will ultimately become mentors themselves.

Episodic Mentoring: Kind of Like Online Dating

How many of us have tried online dating? There are seemingly countless websites where you can go to find "your match." Well, how will you know what your match is? What steps do you go through to make this potential match a reality?

First, you have to do your research: You explore various search engines and find the dating service you want to use. How do you determine that? By price? "Success stories"? Online reviews? Whatever your criteria may be, you have something in mind that will lead you to a particular place.

Once you have chosen your dating service, you create a profile; then you complete a questionnaire (maybe embellishing a few answers), and post a flattering picture of yourself so everyone can see your pleasing face—all of this so the website's fancy algorithm can find your "perfect match."

You submit all your information and the website goes to work. Your email inbox gets flooded with potential matches. Now the real work begins. You need to actually contact the ones who interest you. You read their information, figure out some clever line to say, and go for it.

Does this whole online dating process actually work? For some, maybe; for others, not so much. They may have bad experiences, or perhaps never felt like it was the right fit. But some (the people who write the success stories) get married, have kids and a white picket fence, and presumably live happily ever after.

Compare this to mentoring. Specifically episodic mentoring. What do you have to do? How does dating relate to this? Let's go through the steps and compare.

Doing Your Research

First, you need to do your research and decide where you will seek mentoring opportunities. The law school alumni office? Meet-ups with professors? State or local bar associations? The courthouse? The possibilities are endless. Just like dating service options—and again, all the options can be explored electronically. What motivates you to pick a certain one may be the potential costs involved, or the possibility or probability of success (however you define success for the given occasion), or your interest in what will be going on when you get there. As with a dating service, you are going to have reasons for choosing a specific one.

Once you know where you will be going, you have to create something of a profile. Is this a dinner? A professional meeting? A hearing in court? How should you dress? What will you say? Have an "infomercial" available about yourself (you'll find this a few pages ahead). Have questions ready. Research who will be at the event so you will be prepared.

Pre-thinking the Conversation

First, instead of submitting answers and letting some algorithm do the work, you have to do the work yourself, with some proper advance thinking. What questions do you want to ask? How do you want to start a conversation? Are you going with someone who will be able to introduce you to other people? This is the preparatory work that you must do to avoid appearing frightened, uninterested, or unprepared in front of others. You do not want to come off sounding scripted. But, again, you must be prepared.

Jumping On In

Now comes the real work: You have to go and put yourself out there. Making contact can be the hardest thing to do. Just remember to be yourself, be respectful, and have a good time. It takes a lot to go up to someone and initiate a conversation, but if you are prepared it will work out.

AMY SAYS: A lot of this can be scripted. Just as you say, "Fine, how are you?" in response to the question "How are you?" you can also prepare scripted segues, introductions, "infomercials" about yourself and your interests, and questions to ask the other person.

Let's be honest here, not every first date leads to a second date. Sometimes you say something stupid or get tongue-tied and you never see the person again. So what do you do when that happens? Chalk it up as a learning experience, and get right back out there and try it again. (Read Chapter 10, on negative mentoring, to see what you can learn from a bad experience.)

MATT SAYS: Even if you say something you regret, take the good that you gained, learn from the bad, and make yourself better from it. Not everything that you try in life is going to be a success. Plan for the worst, hope for the best!

Combining Self-Mentoring and Mentoring Episodes

Consider combining self-mentoring with mentoring episodes in which people are present who could positively affect or help you. Put yourself in positions where you will be among professionals, particularly attorneys. Then use the techniques described in this book to learn from them. Observe, question, or engage them in discussion. Make sure the discussion involves something that will help you grow professionally.

Attorneys, like most people, don't mind talking about themselves. They are flattered to be asked and will engage you for at least a question or two. But be careful not to turn a brief mentoring episode into a deposition. Having a question or two in mind that any attorney could respond to will mean you are prepared, whenever you meet someone, to turn the conversation in a direction that might benefit you.

No Pain, No Gain

Is there a cost to mentoring for the protégé? Yes! **You have to actually put yourself out there.** That can be very difficult to do. You have to talk to and listen to people. We all have our strengths and weaknesses. Some people are able to hide those weaknesses better than others. Some people are very self-conscious about what they say or how they say it—to a point where they do not want to talk at all. It can have a paralyzing effect on professional interactions, and sometimes may feel like sheer torture.

MATT SAYS: Thanks to mentoring, I had several great relationships with some of the associate deans at my law school. Who better to know, right? They helped me navigate through law school in the best way possible—knowing what the resources were, taking advantage of them at the right time, and making good decisions.

Mentoring also brought me a job working as a law clerk where I got to write plenty of briefs, petitions, and motions. And I got paid! How did I get this position? I was offered a chance to participate in a 60-minute mentoring session with a local lawyer, and, during our hour together, engaged in a lot of self-mentoring. He found me to be a "bright young man" and offered me a job on the spot. And get this—I almost didn't take it because I thought I had too much on my plate, but another mentor, Dean Timmer, stepped in and convinced me I'd be crazy not to take it.

During law school, I picked up a lot of great advice from my mentors about what to do when I was done—how to get a judicial externship, how to decide where to take the bar, how to decide which type of law to practice, and more. Once you get a taste of how easy it is, you will love it.

For some of us, anytime we step out of our comfort zone, it is an uncomfortable experience.

That is the cost of engaging in mentoring. But, believe us, it gets easier. Just like anything else in life. The more you talk to people, practice interacting, and put yourself out there, the easier it gets. It may almost turn into something fun.

So what's the gain? **The benefit of mentoring is that you will become a better professional, and maybe a better person.** And your way to excellence will be guided by the many people you have in your network. That old phrase is true: It's not what you know, it's who you know.

Where Do I Go?

Once you have prepared yourself with a few self-mentoring questions, it is important to actively seek and take advantage of mentoring opportunities. They exist all around you in law school and the legal world. For law students and new lawyers, think about the following resources for connecting with attorneys:

- Your law school's alumni office.

- The bar association for the state in which you've resided while in law school and the state in which you intend to practice law.

- Local and affinity bar associations. Most counties in the state where you are located likely have a local bar association. You may also find such associations by metropolitan area (like the New York City Bar Association), and by interest and affinity (like the Criminal Defense Attorneys of Michigan and the B'nai B'rith Barristers bar associations). Most of these associations welcome student members and offer free or low-cost membership.

- American Inns of Court. See if a chapter is located in your vicinity and how you can attend as a guest or even join as a law student or young lawyer.

- Legal fraternities. Your law school student bar association may have student chapters of legal fraternities and honor societies such as Phi Delta Phi and Phi Alpha Delta—both devoted to professionalism, ethics, and service. Joining a student chapter may open the door to meeting alumni of these fraternities (ones who are now practicing law or using their J.D.s in their work) who may want to reach out to you as a law student.

- The courtroom. This is a very fertile place to meet attorneys. There you will find lawyers and judges who, at the day's end, may take an interest in who you are and why you've been sitting in the courtroom. If you hope to meet lawyers this way, be sure to wear a suit when you sit in on a trial or motion day.

- The advanced search on Martindale.com. This feature allows you to search by law school, practice area, locality, and other relevant factors.

- And don't overlook the faculty members at your law school. They are all lawyers and may have much to offer you in your professional development.

Following are ideas on how to make the most of these opportunities and possibly turn them into mentoring episodes or, at a minimum, chances to add attorneys to your network.

Court Hearing

If you are going to attend a court hearing, anticipate introducing yourself to the court clerk. Figure out who that person is and, if the time appears right, go up and introduce yourself and say, "I'm a law student [or new lawyer] here to observe." You can bet the clerk will tell the judge, so when the hearing concludes, you want to be prepared for this from the judge: "My clerk tells me you are a law student observing court today. What did you think about what you just observed?" Just be yourself and say what you really think. A natural conversation will probably flow. But before you leave, you will want to ask the judge if you can attend again. For example, ask if there is an especially interesting trial or hearing coming up. Next time you visit, ask the judge if you could pose some questions about what you observe. Write down questions while you observe; in doing so, you are engaging in self-mentoring. And when the judge meets with you later to answer those questions you wrote down, note that he or she is also mentoring you, just by answering your questions.

The idea is that the judge will get to know you and may mentor you for a few minutes. Then you'll have another attorney to add to your network and stay in touch with.

Bar Section Meeting

Let's say you want to attend a bar association section meeting. You are interested in environmental law and the student bar membership is inexpensive, so you decide to join the environmental law section. You are about to attend your first event: It's a regular business meeting of the section and there will also be a presentation. You want to be as prepared as you can be and you don't want to stand out like a sore thumb, so try to make contact with someone before the event. Research who the section chair is and email that person explaining that you just joined as a student and want to attend the event and are wondering how best to prepare for it. The chair will probably be glad to give you some background on the presentation and think it's nice that you want to attend. Maybe there's a proposed state regulatory rule they will be discussing and you can read it. Maybe the presentation is about a particular lawsuit with broad implications for the membership and you can find the pleadings filed electronically and read those.

You get the idea. If nothing else, you are in touch with the chair, who may offer to introduce you to the other attorneys there.

Alumni of Your Law School

If your law school maintains a list of alumni, by all means use it, whether you are still a student or have graduated. Alumni will probably be identified by their type of practice. Knowing their practice area is all you need to make contact. In fact, it's your opening line ("I see you practice personal injury law and I wonder how you like that?") because even if you think you are not interested in their line of work, you may end up changing your mind. Or you may confirm your disinterest. Either decision is an important one.

Once you identify alumni you may want to talk with, either because you want to know more about their practice or because they practice in an area of the country or the type of firm or business you hope to be in, it's time to contact them.

Yes, Even by Email

These days, it's a lot easier to make a "cold call" by email than by phone, or worse, showing up without an appointment. In fact, we recommend email as the best way to reach out to an attorney you don't know and to whom you have no introduction.

Tip: Write a clear subject line, keep the message short, respect their time and don't require a lengthy reply.

Send no more than two short paragraphs. In the first paragraph, explain who you are and how you got his name—for example, "I am a law student at your alma mater and got your name from our alumni list," or "Amy Timmer suggested I contact you." You might also pique their interest by mentioning something you have in common, whether it's a law school or a mutual acquaintance, such as "Professor Timmer is now the Dean of Students and sends her regards," or "Our law school recently won the ABA negotiation competition, placing first in the nation."

In the second paragraph, indicate why you are reaching out and how you will follow up. For example, "I was hoping to talk with you for 15 minutes about how you like practicing personal injury law in Cincinnati and, with your approval, will call your office next week to set up a time for us to talk." Note that you have asked for only a brief reply. The recipient has to do nothing but respond with a simple, "Yes, please call," or "Sorry, my schedule just won't allow for this now." That's the point.

If the attorney says you can call, follow up the next week by contacting his or her office to schedule a time to meet. Say, "I have been in touch with Attorney Smith by email and am calling to schedule 15 minutes to talk with him by phone." If all goes well, you will be added to the schedule without the attorney having to do a thing.

We don't think a phone call is the best way to receive 15-minute mentoring, but if that's all you can do because you are 2,000 miles apart, then that's what you do. Meeting in person is really the ideal. If you are a law student far from the place where the mentor is, then consider traveling to that place on your next break from school. Set up a number of appointments in the area and make it worth your time.

MATT SAYS: Probably the hardest skill to develop is to not talk about yourself. It is one that my wife has taught me to do and that I practice to this day. It is easy to talk about yourself, but not so easy to actually listen to someone else and be interested in what they are saying.

The Ever-Popular Cup of Coffee

If you are seeking an appointment with someone local, offer to buy lunch or a cup of coffee. If you meet at a coffee shop, chances are the attorney will buy his or her own and maybe yours. But you must offer to spring for it, and be prepared to pay, since the attorney is taking time out of his or her schedule for your benefit. If you are asked to meet at the attorney's office, show up with a cup of good coffee and a bagel as an ice-breaker. Your thoughtfulness will be appreciated.

Preparing for Mentoring Opportunities

As mentioned previously, you can get the most out of mentoring episodes by preparing in advance. If you know with whom you will meet, be sure you have researched the attorney and prepared some questions to ask. If you are going to an event where you don't know the attendees, anticipate how you will approach people, what you want to learn, what you might be asked, and what you might say in response. Certainly have your questions ready. Dress appropriately for the occasion, which will usually mean businesswear. Always bring something for note-taking. Bring your business card.

If you are a law student, have your "infomercial" ready (more on that shortly) to briefly explain what you think—at this point in your life—you want to do with your degree.

What Do I Ask?

You can learn something from anyone. The bus driver called "Smooth Jazz" is included in this book's "Dedication" because Matt unexpectedly learned great stuff from daily conversations with him as he rode to school. The trick is to make a list of questions that you can ask anyone, questions that will necessarily help you grow professionally.

Here are some examples to get you started:

- What do you like best about your job? What don't you like?
- What does your best day at work involve? Your worst?
- How do you deal with difficult people?
- What is the most challenging thing you have faced professionally?
- Have you ever encountered an ethical challenge, and how did you deal with it?
- How do you keep your skills up?
- What advice would you give someone who is just starting out?
- How did you get your first job?
- How do you balance your personal life and work life?
- How do you stay healthy?

Begin your questions with "what," "how," or "where," rather than "do you ..." so you will elicit an explanation and not a simple "yes" or "no."

Your "Infomercial"

Have two or three sentences about your career goals ready to tell people when they inevitably ask what you hope to do with your law degree. For example, write down what you already know about what you want to do. You may not know what kind of law you want to practice, or even if you want to use your degree to practice law, but you may know a lot about yourself that will still be helpful for others to know.

- Do you know where in the country you want to live? Which state or climate?
- Do you want to live in a big city or a small town?
- What skills or activities do you enjoy most right now?
- Do you want to work lots of hours in a bigger law firm or more "normal" hours in a government position?

- **You might be able to say something like this:** "I'm not sure yet exactly what I want to do, but I know I want to be in Atlanta. I am willing to work lots of hours because I'm single and just getting started, and I might be interested in owning my own business because I like to work alone and have lots of ambition."
- **Or this:** "I'd like to be in the Northeast in a small town, and I'm interested in public interest law because it's important to me to help give people access to justice. I also like public speaking and love to work as part of a team."
- **Or this:** "My wife and I have two kids, so I know I want to work only a 40-hour week if I can. Our families are in Texas and we'd like to stay near them. Beyond that, I am completely open to what my career might look like."

The Universe Conspires to Help You

Why is your infomercial so important? Well, if you haven't read the 1993 book, *The Alchemist,* by Paulo Coelho ("a fable about following your dream"), then you may not know that if you say out loud what you want, as Coelho phrases it, "all the universe conspires in helping you to achieve it." It's not really magic. Human nature is such that, when you give people something concrete to work with, they almost can't help but offer the assistance you want. So when you say you want to be in Atlanta, a listener is likely to respond, "I know a couple of lawyers in Atlanta I'd be glad to put you in touch with." Or, when you say you want to do public interest law in the Northeast, the listener might say, "Have you thought about the Natural Resources Defense Council? They have an office in New York, I used to have a contact there."

If you are reading this book as a young lawyer, you can surely translate this advice into the type of conversation and questions that will work for you. You, too, can feel free to reach out to attorneys in town, even through a "cold call" email. The point is to create situations where you can learn from other lawyers.

Follow Up, Follow Up, Follow Up

We can't emphasize enough how important it is to follow up each encounter—even a brief one—with an email note. Thank the attorney for talking with you, remind him or her what you talked about and where, and ask if you can stay in touch. Better yet, say you'd like to stay in touch, which does not require a response from the attorney. Then, once every three to four months, send an email reminding the attorney (again) of how you met and what you spoke about. Write about how you are doing in law school, your practice, or your job hunt, and ask nothing of him or her.

Be sure to always share something new about you so the attorney gets to know you better through these communications. The more people feel they know you, the more they can vouch for you and help you. But keep it short—no more than two paragraphs.

That is how you add attorneys to your network. By staying in touch, they will feel that they know you and will be there when you need to ask them for something, and they'll appreciate that you developed the relationship without asking for anything—initially.

CHAPTER 7

MENTEE PERSONALITY TYPES
WHAT IF YOU'RE SHY OR FEAR REJECTION?

As we contemplated putting this book together, Matt started reflecting about himself. Why was he doing this? Why has he liked mentoring? He realized it's the ability to build connections and figure out how he wants to practice and, more important, what he wanted to practice. Some of this book's readers are likely after the same thing. But what if some of you have a hard time talking to people? What if you are shy? What should you do?

First, let's talk about "shyness." What does it mean? Matt has concluded that shyness is an emotion that manifests itself in new situations and makes us feel apprehensive or uncomfortable and hesitant to do things. It can affect our behavior and have a physical manifestation that makes us blush, feel speechless or breathless, have a shaky voice, or all of these, according to various sources. (There's a nice extended definition of shyness and its manifestations at http://kidshealth.org/en/teens/shyness.html.)

Shyness will be intense for some people, and nonexistent for others. Matt once saw a woman give a fantastic presentation but five minutes into it her skin was visibly flushed. Nonetheless, she was confident and very knowledgeable in what she was saying. Her shyness manifested itself physically. Sometimes people associate being shy with not being confident. Not an accurate statement, as evidenced by this woman. She didn't let it bother her, and, therefore, it didn't bother anyone in the room.

Myers-Briggs Personality Types: Introverts and Extroverts

Before we get too far into this topic, we need to take a step back and talk about "personality typology." There are myriad books on this topic, and information on it has been made well-known through the Myers-Briggs Type Indicator test. This test indicates an individual's "personality type."

It's important, when talking about this, to be clear that there is no good or bad, no right or wrong. These are traits that define us all. Unfortunately, society has led us to believe that people who are shy are somehow not as competent as people who aren't shy. Or that extroverts are better than introverts. That is simply not the case!

Moreover, both introverts and extroverts can be shy. The difference is in how they deal with it.

Extroverts

According to the book *Looking at Type: The Fundamentals,* by psychologist Charles R. Martin (first published in 2001), words associated with extroversion include **active, outward, sociable, people, many, expressive, and breadth**. As Martin writes:

> People who prefer extroversion are energized by active involvement in events, and they like to be immersed in a breadth of activities. They are most excited when they are around people, and they often have an energizing effect on those around them. When you are extroverting you like to move into action and to make things happen—extroverts usually feel very at home in the world. With their orientation to the outer world, extroverts often find their understanding of a problem becomes clearer if they can talk out loud about it and hear what others have to say.

Martin also states that extroverts may:

- Be seen as go-getters or "people-persons."
- Feel comfortable with and like working in groups.
- Have a wide range of acquaintances and friends.
- Sometimes jump too quickly into activity and not allow enough time for reflection.
- Sometimes forget to pause to clarify the ideas that give aim or meaning to their activities.

Introverts

According to Martin, words that are associated with introverts include **reflective, inward, reserved, privacy, few, quiet, and depth**. Martin writes in *Looking at Type*:

> People who prefer introversion are energized and excited when they are involved with the ideas, images, memories, and reactions that are a part of

their inner world. Introverts often prefer solitary activities or spending time with one or two others with whom they feel an affinity, and they often have a calming effect on those around them. When you are introverting, you take time to reflect on ideas that explain the outer world—introverts like to have a clear idea of what they will be doing when they move into action. With their orientation to the inner world, introverts often like the idea of something, better than the something itself, and ideas are almost solid things for them.

And Martin further states in the book that introverts may:

- Be seen as calm and "centered" or reserved.
- Feel comfortable being alone and like solitary activities.
- Prefer fewer, more intense relationships.
- Sometimes spend too much time reflecting and don't move into action quickly enough.
- Sometimes forget to check with the outside world to see if their ideas really fit their experience.

Introversion and extroversion also have been associated with people who are shy and those who are not shy, respectively. These are unfortunate misconceptions that have led some people who are shy to think that they might not be as "good" as more outgoing people. They will say things like, "That's just something that I cannot do," or "I'm not outgoing enough to be mentored." Well, guess what? Extroverts can be shy just as much as introverts.

This is simply a matter of how the different typologies deal with their shyness. Extroverts appear to not be shy because, as we discussed earlier, they live in the "outside" world; other people energize them, so naturally they want to be around people. Extroverts speak to help themselves think—their thought process is outside—so you may hear them talking to themselves, which is their way of hearing themselves work through a problem.

As with Everything, Prepare (But Even More So if You're an Introvert)

Introverts often feel drained by people, so when it comes to a possible mentoring situation, they instinctively do not want to go. They tend to feel "de-energized" when it comes to social interactions and, therefore, mentoring seems harder to do. Introverts also tend to think before they speak. While everyone goes through the same process, there is a difference in how or where we do so. As introverts begin to realize that the only difference lies in their flow of information, how can this be useful to them in mentoring?

Introverts will have to plan out the questions they are going to ask. They have to figure out how to feel most comfortable with the situation. They may say to themselves, "I am concerned about having to be spontaneous." This is why they should write questions first. That way they know which ones to ask and will not have to "think on their feet." Clearly, it is not that introverts aren't able to be mentored, or to network; it is more a function of preparation. They need to prepare and make decisions ahead of time about going outside of themselves, and then allow time to re-energize after social events or meetings.

Introverts also must depend on their calendars when getting involved in mentoring. In other words, they must devote specific blocks of time to identifying people whom they want to be mentored by, and then must calendar in time to reach out to those people, by phone or email, or by attending events where they can meet. If introverts don't make the time to do this—and force themselves to do it—they may choose what feels like the easier route of not doing it at all.

Know Thyself

Let's say you know that you're an introvert and that you don't like being in groups of people. Public events are the worst for you, but since this is something you know about yourself, you can plan ahead. If you are getting ready to go to a bar association meeting and know that this is naturally going to be a difficult task for you, prepare your questions ahead of time so you feel put together. One thing that might make you feel more comfortable is that you do not necessarily have to make eye contact. Try looking just above or below the eye line, or at the person's nose. Little tricks like this may help you to be more willing to talk to people.

Now let's say you're an extrovert. You love going to social events and being in contact with everybody. You are going to be the one who moves around the room, stands in one group for a few minutes, then goes to another and says hi. You will work the room! But you also know ahead of time that you have a goal you want to accomplish at the event. You want to be mentored. Yet as an extrovert, you may very likely get caught up in the conversation and forget all about your questions. Because you know this about yourself, you will need to make a list of questions and a list of things you want to accomplish, or even an outline of sorts. If you do not, you are going to go off on tangents.

In other words, use what you know about yourself in the mentoring process. Once you figure out whether you are more introverted or extroverted, use it to your advantage. Introverts should take a lot of notes and let the mentor do the talking. Extroverts must try to refrain from doing all the talking and learn to listen carefully— note-taking helps with that, too.

You see, knowing about yourself is one of the best things you can do for yourself. If you have certain tendencies, or act a certain way, you can plan how to use those to your advantage. You can change your study habits, you can control your social surroundings, you can understand why you feel the way you do in certain situations without feeling bad or confused about it.

When it comes down to it, if you're an extrovert, great! If you're an introvert, great! The most important thing is to learn about you, figure out what works and what does not work for you. And as we hope you have seen, both types need to prepare questions and take notes.

The Go-To Questions

Matt has a few questions that he always likes to ask to find out about an attorney with whom he is talking. First, of course, you must find an appropriate setting, but when you're there, here are some "go-to" questions:

- Why do you like this type of law?
- How did you choose to practice this type of law?
- What is your favorite part about what you do for work?
- What is your least favorite part?
- In your opinion, what is the best thing I should do now to prepare myself to practice?
- What was the best thing that ever happened to you as a lawyer?
- What are your thoughts on mediation?
- Is moot court or mock trial participation important for you to see on a young lawyer's résumé?
- What is something that you like to see on a new graduate's résumé?
- What is the most important thing you look for in hiring a young attorney?
- What is the best career move you have made? The worst?
- How did you find a mentor when you needed one?
- How active is the local bar?

By the way, be sure not to ask personal questions (until the lawyer opens the door to this)—and never assume. Where the lawyer lives, whether he or he has kids, how old the lawyer is, and the like is really none of your business, and such questions can make a person feel uncomfortable. So stay away from the personal stuff.

The Good News

Everyone, regardless of personality type, can try mentoring. You just need to use an approach that is comfortable for you, and come prepared!

CHAPTER 8

THE EPISODIC MENTORING SESSION
THINK BIG VERSUS MINUTIA

Seeing the Big Picture

Before he started his law school adventure, people gave Matt lots of advice. As it turned out, Matt and his wife had a few friends who were either in their last year of law school or had just finished, who communicated with them on occasion. They said that there were lots of details involved in the law, but to always remember to look at the big picture. (Take the law of negligence. The first concepts you learn are very complex—the unforeseeable plaintiff, joint and several liability, *res ipsa loquitur*— but when you take a step back and look at the big picture, it seems rather easy: duty, breach, causation, and damages.)

You should treat mentoring sessions the same way. If you sit down and try to figure out all the little details, you may feel overwhelmed and not want to do it. But if you look at it as a simple conversation, it is not only beneficial, but fun, too! Let's face it: Mentoring takes us out of our comfort zones. It can be intimidating and stressful, but so can being an attorney. We might as well learn how to deal successfully with stress and intimidation now.

Practicing Skills

Earlier in this book, we talked about something called the MacCrate skills. Every time you have a mentoring session or are going to a specific event, look at those skills again to decide which area to work on. Chances are you can always use help in every area. Pick a skill or two and formulate a few questions in your mind. That way you will focus your mentoring session on what you want to get out of it.

For example, if you want to focus on the skill of investigating facts, you may ask a mentor whether he or she had a case that required in-depth fact investigation, and how he or she recognized and tackled the problem. What techniques did the lawyer use to find the facts needed? Document review? Private investigator? Interrogatories or depositions? How do you know which to use? What worked best? Who paid for the investigation? Talking just about this one skill could easily take up an hour of time.

MATT SAYS: You have to remember: All this mentoring "stuff" is to help you gain knowledge, skills, and ethics, to learn about what type of law you want to practice, and maybe even to make connections. We do all of this to set ourselves up for the future.

So, the first big thing you have to do is figure out what you want to get out of the session. It might not always happen, but going in with a game plan will be your best bet to get the result you want.

Keep the Conversation Going

Let's be candid: We all like to talk about ourselves—which includes attorneys. If you ask them a question, they may talk for 20 minutes. But what do you do if they ask you a question? You might be tempted to talk for a long time about that one question. But the skill you need to focus on is sharing information that will help the relationship grow, then shifting the conversation back in the direction you want it to take. You need to become skilled at keeping the conversation going.

Question

Let's say you're talking with a lawyer who has a solo practice, and you are really interested in running your own show. You want to find out how this lawyer accomplished all that he or she has done. But all the lawyer is talking about is bankruptcy law. Look for a moment when you're able to get a question in, and find a way to shift the conversation back to what you want to learn. For example, ask: "How did you get started with your own firm?" "What is your least favorite thing about being your own boss?" "What is the best thing about having your own practice?" You get the idea; your question has to flow with the conversation, but this person can really give you some insight into the very thing you want to do.

No matter what else, always ask, "If you had to do it over again, what would you do differently?"

Developing Your Listening Abilities

Learning from others through conversation is a skill. If you don't have it right now, you can develop it. It just takes some practice. Matt has mentioned "Smooth Jazz," the bus driver, whom he named for the music he played while he drove. Here's how it all began. Matt rode the city bus every day to get to school and, because he is an introvert, he decided to practice conversing and seeking guidance with the bus driver. He started with simple conversation, asking Smooth Jazz how long he had been driving the bus, and so on. Then Matt got into questions that would help him develop professionally. For example, Matt asked him how he dealt with disruptive people and what problem-solving techniques he used. The driver had lots to say on the subject. Matt learned so much from Smooth Jazz that he kept going back to him with questions. Incidentally, Matt also learned that Smooth Jazz has a brother practicing law in the very city in California where Matt wanted to practice—and he offered to introduce Matt to his brother via email when Matt was ready. What a good payoff for one's very first attempt at self-mentoring, and a great example of the universe conspiring to give you what you want.

You can do this with anyone—it does not have to be an attorney or a judge or a bus driver. Just talk to people, find out about them and how they deal with life, and be genuinely interested in what they are saying. Open yourself up to learning from others. Too many times we ask questions just as filler while waiting for our chance to get back in the conversation. When you ask a question, pay attention to the answer and find a follow-up to it. Again, this is why it is a skill—developing it takes practice.

The skill of listening will help you in all areas of life, especially in legal work. When you have clients, they are not going to come to you and want to hear you talk. We have to interview them and find out what the real issue is. Get past the fluff, ask the right questions, and do what they are paying you $200 an hour to do.

Developing this skill will help you with client counseling, mediating disputes, mentoring others, dealing with your boss, and more. Keeping the conversation going is useful in so many ways.

It's Really About Me!

When we speak of mentoring, we have a habit of thinking, "It's not about me (the protégé), it's about them (the mentors)." And this is the appropriate focus for a mentoring session—you are asking the mentor about his or her experience. But after Matt's very successful mentoring episodes, we added: "But it's also really about me!" Why? Because Matt has been able to soak up every bit of useful information he could get from the mentor, which ultimately proves helpful.

In the first meeting with an attorney who has agreed to mentor you, make sure the focus is on the attorney, not on you. As we've said, you can help the mentor get started by coming to the session with a list of questions that will aid your professional growth. (See Chapters 6 and 7 for a list of go-to questions). Now, of course, there will be a "getting to know you" period of the session. Don't hesitate to offer a concise description of yourself and your interests (the "infomercial" described in Chapter 6), but keep it short and steer the conversation back to the mentor. Without being pushy or rude, simply keep the focus on the mentor by asking the questions you need answers to.

In longer-term mentoring relationships, there will be more give-and-take, but when you're just starting out, and trying 60-minute mentoring for the first time, you've got only one hour to learn as much as you can. Approach the situation with the right attitude and you will leave a richer person.

CHAPTER 9

FEEDBACK FROM THE EPISODIC MENTORING STUDY
"IT CHANGED MY LIFE"

The Mentoring Study

As we were wrapping up our mentoring study at Cooley Law School (see Chapter 3), the student participants had an opportunity to meet with a social sciences researcher to talk about their mentoring experiences. Since Matt was in the episodic study group, he was asked about the challenges of episodic mentoring. We share his response here:

> "To be honest, I think the biggest challenge of episodic mentoring is making time. Whether you are a law student, law professor, practicing attorney, stay-at-home parent, or grocery bagger, life is busy. We all feel stresses on our time and we all feel like we are being pulled in a hundred different directions.

> "No matter what people say, life does not get easier. If anything, it gets harder. You get married, have kids, have more kids, get a promotion at work, or lose your job. Regardless, life just gets more hectic as we make our journey. The key is time management! That is why mentoring (traditional or episodic) is hard. We think it's something we'll get around to later. I know I have said to myself,

'I will get to that next week; I have too many other fires to put out right now to worry about that.'

"We have all heard the saying that it is not what you know, but who you know that will get you places. The only way we are going to get to know more people is by putting ourselves out there. You have to go to bar association meetings, local chamber of commerce meetings. In order to have mentoring episodes, you have to put yourself out there.

"If you do not plan for episodic mentoring opportunities, then you will not have them. If you do not have them, you will not get to meet as many people as you would have otherwise, and you might not get that golden opportunity that you otherwise would have had. We have a saying in my house: You make time for the things you want to make time for. I strongly believe that applies to anything in life. We will always find time for something we really want to do.

"Please don't misunderstand me here. I am in no way saying that you need to take an hour a week to schedule 'potential mentoring' or anything like that (although that would be a great approach). What I am saying is that you need to make time to prepare the questions you will ask that will result in your being mentored, and you need to make time in your schedule to attend events. You need to put yourself out there. An attorney I met with told me to get out there and get involved with local chapters. She told me that it is not something that happens right away, but with some persistence you will see some dividends."

More Inspiration

To really pique your interest, and give you some reassurance, we thought it would be helpful to also share what other law students in the episodic mentoring study told us, in their own words. We were gratified to find that students were inspired about practicing, changed their minds about certain things, and generally felt they took something valuable from each mentoring episode.

We learned from these students that, while it wasn't always easy, the episodic mentoring they engaged in was worth the effort. And some even had offers of jobs or externships after just one mentoring episode!

Comments from Students in the Episodic Mentoring Study

Here's our favorite comment, followed by quotes from the participants:

> "Thank you for the opportunity to participate in this important study. It changed my life. I am so much more cognizant of the importance of legal mentors. While I have always been a sort of mentor seeker (I am the baby in my family), I did not realize its true value until I started journaling my experiences during this process. I am better for this experience, and I thank you."

Question 1: What impact did your mentoring relationships have on your decision to become a lawyer?

- **My mentoring relationships let me know that I have much to offer the legal community.** While I have a tremendous amount of learning to do, I feel that I belong in the legal community.

- **The mentoring made me look at whether the field I want to go into is really right for me** or if I should start exploring other fields. But one experience I had really encouraged me and inspired me in the field I want to practice in. It's always encouraging when you meet someone that you can tell just really loves their job and what they are doing. I find that type of episodic mentoring experience the most rewarding.

- **It helped me to realize that intellectual property law is not really the area of law that I desire to practice.**

- **My mentors helped me see the human side of it.** They also helped me see that good attorneys do not get involved in the senseless games that I worry about. Really, they helped me start constructing a solid framework for the way I want my career to be.

- **My mentors showed me that the law truly is a helping profession**, and knowing how much support is out there motivates me.

- **Mentoring helped reinforce that my decision was a great one** by demonstrating some of the benefits of having a J.D.

- **I realized how much lawyers like to hear themselves talk.**

- **I am appreciative because Jeff (one of the mentors) offered me a law clerk position.** He has given me confidence that I can learn the profession and be good at it.

- **Paul (one of the mentors) initially worked as a solo practitioner doing immigration law, and he informed me how difficult it was to do everything on his own right out of law school.** He was actually pretty discouraging! Now he is working at a firm and seems much happier, but overall, I feel that going solo right after school would not be preferable.

- **I asked my mentor about small firms and private practice and he provided a lot of insight.** I like the idea of having freedom in the cases you handle while in private practice, but I also learned that, starting out, there is not a lot of freedom because of the overhead associated with running an office.

- **The attorney I have been in regular contact with is on a completely different career path than I would like to be.** He is part of the Young Lawyers Section of the local bar association and is a fast-rising criminal attorney in Lansing and Chicago. It is nice to see what I do not want to do.

- **Because it's extremely important to find a job in your field that suits you,** this mentoring experience allowed me a special glimpse into the requirements of a tax attorney for the state. Reading a job description is not enough. A mentor shared with me the culture of the work environment, mobility of employment (she transferred around until she found the work she preferred), and what classes were helpful to her in her line of work.

- **The mentoring episode did have an impact on my professional identity.** At first I thought I would open my own practice right out of law school, but after talking to the mentor, I changed my mind. He let me know how important it was to work for others and learn from their mistakes before you do it on your own. He gave me some great advice and I am going to change my plan.

- **My mentor, Janene, told me about her struggles as a law student finding mentors; no one was willing to take the time out of their schedule to speak with her.** She also mentioned her struggles as a recent graduate from law school and how hard it was to get a job. She told me that during law school she clerked at the firm where she works now, and at that time there were no African-Americans employed there. She applied there right out of law school not expecting to get a job. However, she was hired and became the first and only African-American attorney at that office [for a time]. She stated that she did not let race and what others had to say deter her from her dreams. She also told me to be strong and pursue anything I want in life; no one can stop me, only I can stop myself.

- **Mentor Maria told me of her experience dealing with victims of domestic violence and how it has impacted her life.** She explained to me the constant struggles women face when they are trying to get out of an abusive relationship. She told me it will take at least seven tries before a woman actually leaves an abusive spouse. She advised me that entering such a field may be difficult if I am too passionate about it. I have to be able to set my personal biases aside, to learn to let go and move on.... She shared with me that I have the right drive and work ethic to get what I want to accomplish. She also gave me some helpful resources to start the planning process for my project.

Question 2: In what ways did this interaction contribute to your career and personal growth?

- **My mentor told me to take one hour each week and think of big things ... no censoring ... just think big.** I will never forget that.

- **The mentoring made me want to work hard when I am a practicing attorney** so I don't develop a bad reputation in the court system.

- **It was encouraging to see a strong female attorney who clearly loves her job.** She encouraged and inspired me to work hard.

- **It was nice to meet someone with the same philosophy.** It was also encouraging to know that you can have it all if you work hard and know how to balance your life.

- **My mentor is a much respected attorney in our area.** Just being associated with him helps my career. He offered me a job after graduation.

- **These meetings helped me to remember that I don't want to be just another "asshole" attorney**—that approaching every situation with a lawyer's brain is not always the best approach and to remember there is a human element to what I am pursuing.

- **My mentor actually stressed the importance of family and how making that a priority was important.** He told me that I should never define myself as a lawyer, or allow being a lawyer to define me.

- **A judge who mentored me reaffirmed some things that I knew about integrity,** but he also showed me the importance of humility and self-awareness, and the importance of treating all individuals with the same level of respect.

- **It reaffirmed some things I had been hearing at that point,** and helped me to better understand the importance of viewing my profession with an entrepreneurial set of eyes.

- **This mentoring experience helped put into perspective what life would be like practicing in Washington, D.C.,** and how demanding it is while trying to maintain a life outside of work. While what I gained from this particular mentoring experience is probably not what is typically expected, it helped me contemplate what I wanted for the rest of my life. While there is no question that I made the right decision to attend law school and to practice law, I began to question if working in D.C., the land of thousands of lawyers, extreme competition, and far from my family and friends, was really what I wanted for myself.

- **It was extremely beneficial to start the mentoring/networking process earlier in my law school career,** rather than later.

- **I have gained invaluable insight into how I should best go about the job search process.** It also caused me to really contemplate which state to take the bar in, since I plan to practice and live in that place for a majority of my life. Lastly, it has forced me to start the job search process early, which I probably wouldn't have begun until right before graduation because I was so focused and stressed just trying to get through law school.

- **My mentor, Kevin, encouraged me to get through school as fast as possible because a lawyer truly learns the law after school.** He recommended just getting out of school as fast as possible and then working at a firm. He said to make sure that I go someplace where I get a large amount of cases—that is the best way to learn. He didn't waste time—he is very goal-oriented and really gets things done. I love it!

- **After speaking with Elizabeth (one of the mentors), I found myself looking at other areas where my law degree could be valuable,** including checking with the Michigan Senate where I was offered an internship. I was also able to speak with Ross (a lawyer) afterward. It turns out he works in a small firm that was started by four attorneys who left the firm I am currently working in. I took his contact information and sent him my résumé for when a position opens up at his firm.

- **After realizing that I could contact people in the legal community and nothing worse than hearing a "no" would happen, I decided to start making contacts in my hometown.** I handwrote a letter to a judge in my hometown asking if I could stop in and chat with him regarding practicing in a small town. As soon as he received my letter, he called me. We briefly talked and set a day and time to go to lunch. When I arrived at the courthouse, the judge had a few matters that still needed to be dealt with, so he invited me to sit in. He had three people come before him and, sadly, the matters all involved substance abuse in some manner. After court was finished, we went to a local restaurant and proceeded to talk about what it is like for him as a sitting judge in the local community. I reaffirmed what I suspected, that most of the people who come through his courtroom are repeat offenders and most involve alcohol and drugs. Aside from learning various things about his experiences, we talked about non-legal things. His house is two blocks from my parents' house, and in a small community, you tend to know the same people and hear the same things.

- **The advice given to me by Judge C. (one of the mentors) has helped me know more of what to expect as a young lawyer.** Admittedly, it is rather intimidating to know that I will be across the courtroom from many seasoned attorneys who are skilled in their craft. However, with the use of this advice, I know better what will be expected of me in the early years of my career. I feel that honing these "tools" may help to shorten my learning curve as a young lawyer.

- **The professor mentoring me is very open and candid. I want to be like that.** She shared her life and professional experiences with me. I'm learning so much about professionalism by just spending time one on one with her. She is very polite, honest, and sincere.

- **My mentor seems confident that he maintains a standard above the required ethical standard set by the state bar.** However, he admits that this practice has cost him both financially and personally. He seemed to hint at a standard of less-than-ethical behavior among many in their state's legal community. He explained that in a small town, refusing to "play ball" may have its costs. However, he warned that the stain of an ethics violation may be even more costly, especially to a young lawyer looking to further his career. In addition, he warned that no one operates with impunity in the legal profession and unethical behavior is the quickest way to lose your law license.

- **This mentoring episode reminded me that there must be a balance between my professional life and my personal life.** I definitely realize that a shortcoming in one may likely lead to a shortcoming in the other.

- **Legal mentors are valuable to law students in times of crisis.** If I were to hear the same words that were spoken by Professor C. come from my dad, I would have thought, oh, you're being nice, but you don't understand law school. If I were to hear those words from another law student, I would appreciate it, but unless they had that same experience, I would also consider it a nicety. I took it to heart because it came from someone who is a lawyer, received grades, and who grades as well as advises students. I think every law student could benefit from a real mentoring relationship with a professor.

- **When I spend time with my mentor, Mr. D., it strengthens my faith in the goodness of people and inspires me to improve my personal character.** The power of quality mentoring for me has been advancing beyond attaining practical legal skills and advice, to include elevating my character.

- **Ms. L. read my résumé.** After that we chatted casually about the appellate advocacy work practiced at her firm. I shared with her that I enjoyed writing as opposed to trial work and that I don't see myself as a litigator. She related. We found many connections. She offered me a job.

- **I did not expect to create a networking relationship during this mentoring episode.** I went in thinking I'm just going to practice my interviewing skills and have my résumé critiqued. Yet it turned out to be another pleasant and reoccurring theme of this mentoring exercise—building professional relationships.

- **The mentor offered to pass my résumé on to her supervisor** if I would like to apply for an externship. Networking opportunities often present themselves in an episodic mentoring experience. It has been the greatest surprise of this mentoring study.

- **If there is anything I am afraid of right now, it's hurting my reputation.** If you make a mistake in court, it's okay because there is a learning curve. If you make an ethical mistake or act unprofessionally, it's more difficult to recover. During our second mentoring meeting, Professor V. explained now that I am no longer in her class we could be friends. She also sent me a personal invitation to attend an ethics symposium. The invitation stated that I was invited because I exhibited a high professional standard while in her class, and for demonstrating an interest in ethics. My experience with episodic mentoring has been wonderful—I was surprised that so many wonderful things can come from one encounter. Now that I am aware of this, I seize every opportunity to have an encounter. Being mentored by Professor V. inspires me to set very high standards for my professional identity. This mentoring episode also heightened my awareness about guarding against professional complacency.

- **Mr. D. offered his mentoring assistance anytime I'd like and encouraged me to develop other mentoring relationships, too.** I really responded to his sincerity. He truly wants to help me develop as a young attorney and make a positive impact in our community. When I share the same values with a mentor, it strengthens my sense of self, which in the throes of law school is much appreciated.

- **My mentor gave me some very helpful tips to help me get prepared to be a litigator.** She told me all the classes I should take that will help me with feeling more comfortable speaking in public. She also advised me that the key to success in law school was good time management. She told me to keep a daily schedule, so that I will become very organized and stay on track. She told me to budget well and start saving for graduation because finding a job can be tough. She also told me what bar review course I should take.

- **The interaction was great for my personal growth.** As a student who didn't do as well in Research and Writing class, I felt as though my chances of getting hired were less. I felt great when a mentor informed me that it is not as important as it seems, and that there are many other skills that firms look for. As he listed them, I felt like I possessed all the characteristics he was looking for.

Question 3: How would you describe the strengths of episodic mentoring?

- **The mentoring episode gave me more confidence** than I originally anticipated it would.

- **You get to talk to a lot of different people and get a lot of different views.** Episodic mentoring encourages asking questions and hearing different perspectives.

- **It provided me with various creative ways to make networking contacts** regarding externships, jobs, and advice about the legal profession.

- **The episodic mentoring experience was invaluable** in helping me to figure out exactly what area of law I really do want to practice and in what geographic location and size of law firm.

- **It gives access to a lot of different viewpoints and individuals.** It can create a network of people who, if kept in contact with, can lead to help in the future.

- **The strength of episodic mentoring is that you are able to have many mentors,** which allows you to have different mentors to help with different phases of your career or life.

- **It taught me how to network and how to handle disappointment** when my networking goals have not been met.

- **I found that I was more apt to listen.** Knowing that the encounter might only last a few minutes, I found myself more focused on what the mentor had to say. It helped me become better able to extract the information I was looking for while at the same time being alert to pearls of wisdom I might not have been specifically seeking. The best part is that such encounters can be spur-of-the-moment; you might randomly meet someone at a cigar shop, strike up a conversation, and leave with some great new insight.

- **Episodic mentoring is easy; you can do it anytime, anywhere.** I think it is easy reaching out to lawyers because they want to make the profession better, and they understand law students need mentoring.

- **The best part about it is you get to pick and choose who you want to be having an episodic moment with.** It allows you to broaden the skills you are trying to develop. It is more flexible than being randomly matched with someone. It also helps to work on your communication skills in networking.

- **One of the strengths of episodic mentoring is the lack of time constraints.** This was valuable in my situation as I observed many of those willing to engage with me as mentors to be extremely busy in their professional lives. Also, admittedly, I was rather hesitant to engage prospective mentors at the beginning for fear of being turned away or being considered a nuisance. Episodic mentoring allowed me to feel out the prospective mentor and determine if they would be willing to partake in the session. Thus, this aspect of episodic mentoring was also very beneficial.

- **One personal goal of mine is to develop networking skills.** I gained confidence from striking up a conversation with someone I didn't know, who told me at the end of our conversation that I would make a great prosecutor because of my willingness and ability to talk to people I don't know. He said that is a quality that good lawyers possess, engaging people they don't know. He said he enjoyed our conversation, which improved my confidence. Networking by talking to professionals I don't know is a skill I work at. While uncomfortable at times, I force myself to engage people because I understand the value of mastering this skill.

Question 4: How would you describe the weaknesses of episodic mentoring?

- **There isn't the traditional mentoring session, so once you speak to someone you might not hear from or speak to them again.** There also isn't the opportunity to really get to know someone that you would find in a traditional setting. This form is also harder for shy people because they have to interact with a lot of different people as opposed to getting to know and talk to one person.

- **It is very close to the concept of traditional networking.** But by focusing on short, one-time encounters, there is little help on deeper, more serious issues, and there is less time to really learn from a mentor. It is harder to address serious issues and bigger problems. Less long-term development occurs.

- **The weaknesses of episodic mentoring are that there are no requirements, and you are on your own to meet possible mentors.** It is much harder to create relationships with your mentors, which in turn creates a sense of accountability to meet with them.

- **It depends on the setting in which you have met the person; your experience may not turn out to be positive.** For example, if you meet a mentor through a program of your local bar association, the relationship you are hoping to build or the advice you are seeking may not be genuine.

- **Sometimes you can't reach the person you want to meet with.** Or they are too busy to meet with you. You must always be outgoing and actively searching for some of the mentors. The mentoring opportunity usually doesn't arise unless you initiate it yourself. If you have limited connections, you might not be able to find the episodic mentor you were looking for.

As with everything in life, episodic mentoring has its good and bad points. We shared some of these perspectives from study participants to give you an inside view of the good that can come from mentoring, even when it occurs in just one meeting.

As our students discovered, it's important to ask for guidance from everyone you meet. Most people have something to offer that you can learn from—you just have to ask and listen. And remember that your ultimate goal may still be to find and create the kind of long-term traditional mentoring relationship you can nurture for a lifetime.

CHAPTER 10

WHEN MENTORING GOES BAD

WHERE ARE THE TAKEAWAYS?

Not every mentoring session is going to be successful. Have no fear! You can still take something away from a bad experience—maybe even more than from a good experience. Matt's very first mentoring experience with an attorney at his office was not pleasant, but the next one was good. Here's his story which Matt also shared as part of the episodic mentoring study discussed in the previous chapter.

Basics: Don't Be a No-Show

First, the other student that I was scheduled to be mentored with showed up at the wrong time, so the attorney was not in a good mood to start with. Then when it was the correct time for us to meet the same student showed up late. Do not waste the time of the attorney you are meeting with.

Did I Say Something Stupid?

The meeting started with the attorney walking us back to his office. The first thing he said was, "Do either of you know what we're supposed to do?" I waited for a second and said, "We're here to talk about you!" He did not seem pleased with my response. I was not sure if that was because of what had happened earlier, or the fact that he was talking to two law students.

After things finally started going, he reached over to a shelf on the wall and pulled down a phonebook. I thought to myself, this can't be good. For the next hour, he flipped through this phonebook and talked about his past cases. The whole hour, he kept flipping page after page. I didn't know why.

During the last five minutes he looked up and said, "Well, do you guys have any questions?" It was literally the first opportunity I had to say anything. I asked him one of my prepared questions and he gave me a 30-second answer. That was that. It was not exactly what I had hoped for.

I later realized this was a good experience even though my mentor was not really into it. The stories he told about his cases all had valuable information sprinkled throughout. Even though I did not get an opportunity to ask questions, or steer the conversation the way I wanted to, I was still able to find some gems in there. So, the moral of this story is, there is always a silver lining. Also, be prepared to explain episodic mentoring to your mentor!

Was I Prepared?

Here is something else that I learned: It is quite obvious when you are not prepared for something, whether while getting called on in class, in a job interview, or at a mentoring lunch. No matter what your event is, there is always some preparation that needs to happen before you go.

It's All in the Cards

Over one of my breaks, I had an opportunity to go to a mixer for graduates of my law school who were in the Los Angeles area. There were only about a dozen of us, but I would guess that just seven people had business cards. Writing down your information on a piece of paper does not exactly scream "professional." Even if you are a law student, having your own business card is a must. I love being able to give out my card, because it has details I want someone to know about me right there. It is easy to keep track of and looks professional.

To me, having a business card ready is something simple you can do in advance that will help you succeed in the future. How often do you meet an insurance salesperson who does not have one on them? The minute you ask them what they do, they pull a card out of their pocket and give it to you. It's as if they set you up by asking what you do and when you politely ask the same in return, boom! There it is; they have an open door to tell you about insurance, never failing to say, "Here is my card!"

If you step back and think about it, law students are the same way. We want everyone to know we're students, when we plan on graduating, and how great we will be as attorneys. What better way is there to have someone remember you than by giving them your card? Something like that has the potential to leave a lasting impression.

Was My Mentor Just Not That Interested in Me?

While the Cooley mentoring study was going on, I had an opportunity to meet with a particular attorney. I was really excited about it, and made extensive arrangements to get to his office. (It was winter and freezing outside, and I didn't have a car). When I got to his office, he was not there! My mentor was a no-show and, to make it worse, I was at his office!

His legal assistant looked at me and said: "Oh, he didn't call you?" The first thing I blurted out was, "Uh, nope." She smiled and apologized, explaining to me that he was in court in Detroit and would not be returning to the office that day. She re-scheduled my appointment for a few weeks later and we left it at that.

Weeks passed and the day before I was supposed to go back, his legal assistant called me to cancel again! I could not believe it—was he really that busy? Was my luck that bad? Why did this guy keep canceling on me? These questions were running through my head when she asked me, "Do you want to give it one more try?" Hesitantly, I told her I did and she told me that she knew he was going to be in the office on a certain day because he already had some other appointments set up.

This time, the day before our scheduled meeting, I did not get a call, but decided to call the office to double check that he was going to be in. He picked up the phone. Of course, I did not know it was him, so I asked for him by name and he said: "This is he." I did not know what to say. I had never spoken with him and I absolutely froze! I said, "Uh … hi, Mr. ___, my name is Matt Cristiano, I have an appointment with you today at 3 o'clock and I just wanted to check that you were going to be there, uh, I mean in the office." I don't think he picked up on his past no-shows, because he simply said, "Yes, I'm here; I will see you at 3."

I felt like an idiot! Here it was a few hours before I was going to meet with this guy, and I felt like I had opened my mouth and nothing but stupid came out. I was so embarrassed that I showed up just hoping it would not be like my other experience, where the attorney simply talked on while flipping the phonebook. Things turned out not to be nearly as bad as I had anticipated. We had a good session, I asked my questions and learned a lot.

My First Tussle with Ethics—I Win!

At my first legal job during law school, I was nervous as all get-out. The first day came and I was just thankful I remembered how to tie my tie. As I was being shown around the office, I asked the legal assistant what they used for research. She said, "We just use the law clerks' Westlaw or Lexis." This was a big red alert for me, because that's one thing that is taught to us: Unless it is a school activity, like an externship for credit, we are not allowed to use our student accounts for those research databases, which are free to students.

So, on my first day I found myself in an ethical dilemma. What should I do? If I told my supervising lawyer I couldn't do free research for him, I'd lose my job. The answer actually was easy, because I knew what I had to do. I was not going to risk a character and professional fitness problem before I ever even graduated. It was more a question of how and when to address the issue with him.

The short story is I spoke with my boss and told him I could not use my student password for Lexis or Westlaw while I was being paid by him for this job. To my great dismay, he told me that none of the clerks he had hired before had complained about it, so why wasn't I willing to do it? It was uncomfortable, but I stuck to my position, knowing that I might lose my first legal job on the very first day. I wasn't sure if I was going to keep my job, but I was glad I did the right thing.

The story has a good ending. Let's just say Westlaw is now used at the firm and they have their own account. But it was surely an uncomfortable situation that tested me at the start about how tough things can be.

Looking back, though, I realized that mentoring had paid off for me once again. Ethics were emphasized heavily at my law school and my professor in Personal and Professional Responsibility pounded them into my head. And other mentors, including the two deans I took the professionalism course with, had asked us to write a code of conduct we would stick by in times of trouble. So I did what I knew I had to do and didn't lose my job. But it would have been okay even if I had lost the job. Thanks to my mentors, I know it's better to have your ethics intact than to have a job that will ruin them.

What Can We Take Away from This Experience?

As you can see, each of my negative experiences taught me something useful—stick to my ethics, try my hardest, confirm appointments, have a business card ready. The message is that you, too, can find something useful from every experience, even if it's what *not* to do. Live and learn.

CHAPTER 11

KEEPING IN TOUCH WITH MENTORS
RELATIONSHIP MAINTENANCE

This One's a Keeper

In this book, we have sometimes analogized the mentoring relationship with dating. Well, just as with a few good dates, there will be a few good mentors out there for you. You will click with those people. Their advice will strike a chord in your heart or mind. You will remember their words when you're in a tight spot. You'll think of them when you encounter a dilemma.

Mentors will have the same experience. They will see the impact of their guidance and know they have a protégé they can relate to, get along with, and teach something to. Mentoring has payback for mentors—they may discover a person who is truly interested in learning from what they have to say, or they may discover their next employee.

When the two of you click, keep the relationship going. Most of the work of sustaining the relationship, frankly, is up to the protégé. Certainly the mentor should offer to be available to the protégé and may say something as simple as, "Let's stay in touch." The protégé should grab onto that opportunity and not let go.

Sporadic but Regular Communication with Mentors

Here's what mentors want: They love to hear from their protégé when the protégé doesn't need them. But they don't want to hear a lot and they don't necessarily want to reply. So protégés should think about sending a short email to their mentors every quarter or so, keeping them updated on what is happening in the protégé's life.

Write a couple of paragraphs to the mentor. Tell about the classes you are currently taking, a new skill you learned or an experience you had in court. Make it fun and interesting. Ask about the mentor without really requiring a response. Mention something the mentor told you that you took to heart. This will show that those comments resonated with you. Use this kind of expression: "I hope you are doing well and haven't had any more trouble from that rude opposing counsel you told me about."

Three or four months is a minimum amount of time that should pass before you send another update. There may be lots to tell in the life of a law student or new lawyer that the mentor will find interesting. End each email with a wish for the mentor's continued good health, and say that you'll be back in touch in a few months. That's it.

If the mentor wants to write back, you've opened the door. If he or she doesn't have time, the mentor won't feel that he or she is being rude by not responding because you clearly crafted your email to not require a response.

AMY SAYS: It's a little disappointing when a former student or protégé contacts you out of the blue—five years later—and asks for help. They write emails that start out, "Sorry I haven't stayed in touch, but can you help me with ...? So to this day, I still stay in touch with my mentors from practice (now 25 years ago), even if it's just a call during the holidays. It's fun. We may not have a whole lot to say to each other, but we get caught up and enjoy the 15-minute call or email. And guess what? I'm now (still) learning from them as they tell me how they are winding down their careers.

Deposits Before Withdrawals

When you stay in touch this way, your mentor will be there for you when you need them. And that day will probably come. So the idea is to keep the relationship alive so no catching up is required when you do have a question or need help.

It's really just common courtesy. Staying in touch is the deposit you make in the professional relationship account. Make as many as you can before you make a withdrawal—i.e., ask for a favor—so that your request will be warmly received. Remember that you are not likely to get through practice without asking for help along the way.

Lifelong Learning

Mentors can help you every step of the way throughout your practice and life. Just as Amy is now learning from an elderly aunt about how to run a household when you have bad arthritis—something she'll inevitably need to know—you can always learn from those who have already dealt with the same thing you are going to have to deal with at some point.

Some mentors can be there to listen when you are considering a job change. Some can offer specific help with a case you are working on because they've had a similar one. Some can continue to introduce you to people you need to know or send work your way. Some can push you to take on pro bono cases once your career is thriving. And some could even pass their entire business along to you when they retire.

If you are lucky enough to establish a strong professional relationship with another attorney, don't let it just fade away. The benefits of staying in touch are legion.

PART 3

FOR
MENTORS

CHAPTER 12

HOW TO BECOME A MENTOR
HELPING OTHERS

Giving Back: The Mentor's Perspective

Call it ego gratification, call it teaching, call it giving back—whatever you call it, it feels so good. As we age, our perspective on life changes, from focusing on ourselves to passing on to others what we've learned along the way. It's a natural human instinct to do this—it's one of the consequences of being social animals. Mentoring allows us to give back in a way that not only helps young lawyers, but also improves our profession. Lawyers have a vested interest in helping other lawyers develop into good professionals—it improves the system for all of us.

We all reach that point where we have something to offer to others. Even newer lawyers—those just a few years in practice—have something to offer to those less experienced. And the act of offering is fulfilling.

Costs

There are certainly costs involved in mentoring, primarily the time it takes to do it. But you will find in reading this book, especially the earlier chapter on types of mentoring, that mentoring can be done in ways that won't take more time away from you than you are willing to offer. In other words, **the cost of mentoring is affordable**.

AMY SAYS: I became a law teacher because when I was practicing law, the best day I had all week was when I volunteered to teach a Legal Methods class at my law school. I felt this wonderful sense of accomplishment, of making a difference. When I was a litigator, I often felt like all I did was move money from one corporation to another. Teaching had much more meaning for me and allowed me to see the positive impact I could have on others. Now that I spend more time on administrative matters than teaching, mentoring gives me that same satisfaction.

Finding Fulfillment

We are all searching for fulfillment in our lives. If your job isn't bringing you the feeling that you are making a difference, or if your non-working life feels somewhat meaningless or self-centered, you might find the fulfillment and meaning you seek by looking outside yourself and helping someone else. Sure, you may say, "I'm a lawyer and I help other people for a living." But if the stress of that work and the constant demands on your time leave you feeling empty or exhausted, mentoring may be something that will soothe your soul.

There are lots of reasons to mentor law students and new lawyers, and we'll run through those in the following pages, but for now let's talk about what most mentors say: **The very best thing about mentoring is that it leaves them feeling fulfilled.** You've spent a lifetime learning your craft and learning about life. You have so much knowledge and experience that law students and young lawyers would be thrilled to hear about. Something magical happens when you share that knowledge, for no other purpose than to share it. It feels good. It feels right. It makes you want to go home with a smile on your face.

Finding the Time

When Amy first came up with the program, "60-Minute Mentoring," everything changed. Suddenly plenty of lawyers were willing to be mentors. They were liberated by the idea that they didn't have to make a huge or extended commitment of time. When the program began at the law school, every lawyer we asked said, yes, they could find an hour to meet with a law student to talk about professionalism and career issues. **Everyone can find an hour.**

By the way, you can mentor in five minutes, even in one sentence. (Recall the law student who got himself mentored via Twitter, asking well-known legal professionals to give him their best career advice in 140 characters.) The trick is to remember that **whenever you talk with a law student or a new lawyer about lawyering and life balance, he or she is soaking up everything you say.** You are mentoring whether you know it or not. Don't forget, momentous things can happen in a moment, and every moment can matter to a protégé.

This is not to discount those who prefer connecting with one person for a significant amount of time to focus their mentoring efforts on developing that person's skills, ethics, and knowledge. If that's what you prefer and you have the time, there is probably no better mentoring than that!

A Teaching Opportunity

Lawyers have to be good teachers because teaching is at the very heart of what we do. If you like that part of your job, mentoring is for you. Mentoring at its essence is passing along the knowledge, experience, and wisdom you've gained over a lifetime.

You'd be surprised how many law students would be excited to learn about what you consider the minutiae of your work. They also want to know how you balance your work and your life. Trust us: Even before they graduate, law students are quite aware of the amount of time they will have to dedicate to their work. They wonder how their spouse or significant other will understand. They wonder if they'll have time for their families. They need to be told that they are in charge of their lives and will have to protect those relationships. They need to know that it can be done.

It Feels Good

Even if you aren't inspired to do good for others, you may be surprised how good it makes you feel. When someone thanks you, sincerely, for the time you've spent with them, you experience a psychological lift. Your attitude improves. You may even begin to see a larger connection between human beings.

You Can Learn Some Things Yourself

Do you think you can't learn from a protégé? Think you know it all? Let us suggest that you don't. Protégés can teach you about the world from their perspective, which we guarantee is not your perspective. They have skills older lawyers don't have, especially related to technology. Thanks to Matt's experience with a legal employer who still didn't have Westlaw, that firm now has an account. Matt even introduced them to ways of storing their files electronically. The longer he worked there, the more they realized they could learn from him. And protégés have life experiences that are likely nothing like yours. Considering they'll be running our country one day, it wouldn't hurt to get to know them.

If your protégé is different from you—in age, race, experience, culture—imagine what you can learn from that person that will help you better understand your clients or jurors, or the world around you.

Improving the Profession

Do you think you're a better lawyer after 20 to 40 years of experience than you were when you were just starting out? Sure you are. Do you think the lessons you've learned in life and about life could help a new lawyer be a better lawyer or better person? You bet they could.

We know our profession could use some improving. Many state supreme courts are now requiring new lawyers to be mentored for a year (or more) by seasoned lawyers. (See the National Legal Mentoring Consortium website at www.legalmentoring.org for a good list of mentoring programs nationwide.) So we have definitely figured out the connection between mentoring and improving the profession. Now you can be a part of that, too, as much as your time allows.

It's the Community, Silly!

You operate in a legal community, whether it's local, statewide, or national or worldwide. You may want to perpetuate or improve the tenor and collegiality of that community. Mentoring allows you to play a part in doing exactly that.

Imagine the opportunity you have to be a role model for a new attorney joining your legal community. Do you want them to understand the values by which that community operates? Do you want them to know the importance of such things as civility and respect for others? Then show them and teach them, and warn them, if you have to. These will be the attorneys with whom you may work daily or occasionally. If you find yourself complaining about the inappropriate behavior or values of newer attorneys, this is your chance to change that. Mentoring is a powerful way to shape the incoming group of attorneys concerning the ways of your community, and thereby perpetuate the good environment you have already achieved.

Giving Back

Then there's the realization that creeps up on us as we get older—we have a whole lot of good stuff to impart to others. And what amazing resources we have to pull from to bring others along. Our knowledge, skills, ethics, opinions, experiences, wisdom, and ideas are the sustenance that hungry new lawyers and law students are craving. They may be afraid to ask. So make it a point to offer those things by being a mentor.

AMY SAYS: I think it was around my 45th year that I started adding the role of "counselor" to my dean of student's duties. I began to see what a positive impact I could have by simply offering guidance, comfort, or advice to a troubled, lost, or questioning person, on top of whatever other information they came to me for. What a difference that made in my relationships with them.

Expanding Your Legacy

If you're at least in your 50s, you may have begun to think about the mark you will leave on this world. **Mentoring is one way to have a lasting impact—through influencing the life of another.** Your teachings, advice, and modeling can have a lasting impact on a mentee, who will keep your lessons alive.

Making the Connection

If we have convinced you to want to do this, there are many ways to connect to a mentee. If there's a law school nearby, contact them and ask to be added to their list of mentors. Every law school out there is looking for you. If you are comfortable Skyping, using Google Hangouts, or mentoring by phone or email, you can make yourself available to your alma mater or any other law school of your choice.

Many local and affinity bar associations offer mentoring programs. These are commonly of the traditional, matched-pair type, and may therefore offer the opportunity to get to know your mentee well and help that person throughout his or her career.

Contact your state bar to see if it operates a statewide mentoring program. The states that now require mentoring for new lawyers will definitely want to know you are interested.

If you are a member of a law firm or law office that recently hired a new lawyer, that lawyer could use your help, even though he or she may be uncomfortable asking for it. Reach out and take that person under your wing. You, the mentee, and the office will all benefit.

In the past five years, there has been an upsurge in county, local, and affinity bar association mentoring programs. They are discovering that new attorneys especially crave this service from their local bar. So call them up and volunteer to be a mentor to a new attorney or law student in your legal community.

You Have Everything You Need

All you need in order to mentor a lawyer or law student is yourself and a willingness to share. Actually, you may be mentoring a new lawyer without even realizing it simply through your behavior. New lawyers and law students want to know what you know. It's as simple as that.

If all else fails to convince you, just try it out. You've only got an hour to lose, and who knows—it might turn out to be one of the best things you ever did.

CHAPTER 13

MENTOR PERSONALITIES AND APPROACHES
LAWYER, KNOW THYSELF

Type Doesn't Matter

The most important thing in this chapter to say right up front is that **your personality type doesn't matter—any attorney can provide mentoring.** You may be more comfortable mentoring in ways that differ from what you may think is the standard mentoring relationship, and we encourage that.

If It Doesn't Work, You've Only Lost an Hour

We begin this chapter by appealing to the mentoring skeptics, because the rest of you are already on board. We have already liberated you from the notion that you have to spend lots of time with your protégé, because we are promoting 60-minute professionalism mentoring and, therefore, asking for only an hour of your time. What you will do with that hour is entirely up to you. We can promise that any new lawyer or law student will appreciate just being around you for that time.

Remember the Mentee

The mentee will probably be intimidated by you to some extent. Put them at ease. Offer them a cup of coffee. Maybe come out from behind your big imposing desk and sit with them at a smaller table. Meet in a coffee shop. **Just keep in mind that you are perceived as intimidating, and try to break down that perception to invite real conversation.**

If You Like to Talk, Start There

A one-hour discussion with a new mentee—one whom you may not see again—really should be crafted by you and the mentee. You need not spend time "telling each other about yourselves," because time is limited, but you should start with deciding what the mentee would like to talk about. So you must begin by asking what the mentee hopes to gain from the one-hour discussion.

A shy mentee may throw out a topic that really isn't the one he or she wants to focus on, but that's okay because you have to start somewhere. If you are using professionalism as your mentoring theme, the mentee will likely ask you generally what role ethics and professionalism have played in your professional life. You can also review the questions at the back of this book that we suggest mentees ask, so you can give some thought to those in advance.

Jump in and share your thoughts. Tell a story. Get personal and talk about whether and how you integrate your own values with professional rules of conduct. Do they ever conflict? What do you do when that happens? Or go a different direction and talk about behaviors you have observed that have gotten lawyers into trouble. We often tell mentors this is not a time to relate war stories, though that is not necessarily true. But consider that your goal is to share something with the mentee that may help in his or her career.

The key is to bring the mentee into the discussion, so do that as you go. This is not a time to intimidate the mentee by using the Socratic method. But it is a time to understand what he or she is seeking from you in that hour. If the mentee doesn't know, just take the conversation where you want to. The mentee will catch up.

So You Don't Want to Spend an Hour Talking

Everyone says lawyers like to talk. But not all of them do. Mentoring requires more than talking, but you can start there. If you don't want to spend the bulk of your time talking, take mentees to court with you. Let them sit in on a client interview or watch a mediation. Take them to a business or bar meeting. Simply let them observe what it is you do that is observable. But make time to talk about *what* they observed. They will have questions.

If you use this method of one-hour "mentoring through observing," you may want to plan a second meeting to talk about what happened. And, by the way, second meetings are not only not prohibited, they are encouraged.

Can We Go Beyond Professionalism?

Absolutely! The reasons we suggest you **start with professionalism mentoring** are because:

- It is important to our profession.
- It is always understandable to a mentee without too much explanation.
- And any attorney can talk about it with any protégé.

Still, if you decide to take the conversation into career exploration, or discuss what your practice is all about or how you got into it, go for it—but only if the mentee asks for that.

Know Thyself

If you think one-hour mentoring is an opportunity to tell someone else how smart or important you are, we don't want you to mentor. However, we also recognize that the lessons you offer may have that result, and that's okay. Just don't make blowing your own horn the theme of the mentoring session.

We're keeping this chapter short because we don't want to lay out too many rules or procedures for episodic mentoring. The point really is just to start a conversation.

CHAPTER 14

A TEMPLATE FOR PROFESSIONALISM MENTORING
HOW DO I DO THIS?

What Mentees May Ask of You

So that you feel prepared for your first mentoring session, it is only fair that we share what we told mentees they could be talking about with you. First, we suggested the protégé should work toward gaining certain skills and characteristics. You can talk about these things openly and directly, or you can model them, but these are the things protégés ought to be asking about or observing in you:

Characteristics of a successful professional:
- Personal ethics including honesty and candor
- Dedication to thorough research and excellent work product
- Civility
- Inquisitiveness
- Patience
- Open-mindedness
- Dependability
- Preparedness
- Cultural competency (how to understand others)
- Sociability
- Integrity (doing the right thing when no one, or when everyone, is watching)

Skills and abilities required of a lawyer:

- Problem-solving
- Legal analysis and reasoning
- Legal research
- Factual investigation
- Communication
- Counseling
- Negotiation
- Alternative dispute resolution
- Litigation
- Organization and management of legal work
- Recognizing and resolving ethical dilemmas
- Dealing with difficult people
- Handling a budget
- Running a meeting
- Creating a successful agenda
- Inspiring others to be their best
- Strategic planning
- Managing people, including focusing their work on a strategic plan
- Billing clients
- Marketing

In addition, you should know that, as a mentor, the heavy lifting is not all up to you. Mentees really should be coming to you with specific questions of their own. So that you can think ahead about what they might ask you, here is a sampling of things we suggested they ask in this book's section for mentees:

- Why do you like this type of law?
- How did you choose to practice this type of law?
- What is your least favorite part about this area of law/having your own business/working here?
- What is your favorite part?
- What is the best thing I should do now to prepare myself to practice?
- What was the best thing that ever happened to you as a lawyer?
- What are your thoughts on mediation?
- What are some things that you like to see on a new graduate's résumé?
- What is the most important thing you look for in hiring a young attorney?
- What is the best career move you have ever made?

- Your worst career move?
- How did you find a mentor when you needed one?
- How active is the local bar?

Their Ideas on How You Might Help Them

Lastly, we offered mentees some ideas on how a mentor can help a protégé, should the mentoring episode lead to other episodes or a long-term mentoring relationship. **We do not want mentors to be concerned that mentees will ask them for a job after a one-hour session.** Protégés absolutely should not be using 60-minute mentoring for such a purpose. If they do, they should be instructed about their mistake. We told protégés that you, the mentor, could:

- Help with specific concerns about law school or lawyering.
- Expose mentees to the legal world through shadowing and discussion.
- Supervise them in pro bono work or have them join you for public service work.
- Discuss legal issues that they need help with and share your knowledge about areas of law.
- Educate them about a specific practice area.
- Describe how you balance work and personal life.
- Share professional experiences and insights that will help mentees grow.
- Be a role model for appropriate and professional behavior.
- Teach them what you know about professional conduct and development.
- Talk about their professional development plan and review the mentee's professionalism portfolio.
- Introduce them to people who employ their law degrees in ways that interest the protégé and help them develop a network of attorney contacts.
- Teach them about ethics challenges and how to handle them.
- Review the mentee's résumé and cover letter and write a letter of recommendation.
- Conduct a mock interview with the mentee.
- Make introductions to people who are looking for externs or employees.
- Advise them on how to make a successful transition from law student to bar examinee to attorney, and about both the good moves and the mistakes that you made in the process.
- Attend professional events together, such as bar association meetings.
- Allow them to do some legal research or writing for you.

If your protégé comes to the meeting empty-handed, you now have a number of ideas for what you can talk about and for how you might help mentees develop their professional stature and identity.

Rules of Professional Conduct

The rules of professional conduct provide fertile ground for professionalism mentoring. Many mentees will have already studied the rules in a law school course, but a review or, better yet, a story or two about how the rules come to life in practice will not hurt.

As a mentor, you may have experience with particular rules due to cases you have handled, or bar work you have engaged in, that will help bring those rules to life for the mentee. Without reference to particular cases or rules, you may want to engage in a general discussion about the lawyer's duties to the client, the public, the profession, and the legal system.

Observations of Lawyer Incivility

You may have directly witnessed lawyer unprofessionalism, or you have likely heard about it in more well-known cases. You can find examples online, and you may also get information from various sources including the American Board of Trial Advocates (ABOTA) Civility Matters program. That program uses deposition videos, transcripts, and court films to show various types of misconduct that will prompt a discussion of everything from swearing and fist-fighting to other, less flagrant ways of antagonizing an opponent. While some of the behavior is shocking, it represents how emotional law practice and advocacy can become and, therefore, how prepared a lawyer must be to deal appropriately with the passions that can arise. You might show these video clips to your mentee and discuss them. Or you can talk about how you have been challenged in certain circumstances to keep your own emotions in check and how you accomplished that.

Ethical Challenges That Lawyers Might Face

It's hard to practice law without encountering ethical challenges, so mentors may have personal experiences to share that exemplify how to act ethically. If you haven't had such experiences yourself, you can easily find examples of unethical behavior in the databases of attorney grievance commissions' or discipline boards' publicized orders of discipline. Also, mentors can review with mentees the orders of discipline listed in their monthly state bar journals.

It's important to emphasize to mentees that they must not only be ethical when no one is looking—i.e., when they might think they can get away with unethical behavior—but also when everyone is looking, which may include having to report the misconduct of another attorney.

You might also want to discuss the slippery slope of failing to be excruciatingly ethical at all times and in all decisions. The choice to pad hours billed to a client by even five minutes can lead a young lawyer to add 15 or 20 minutes the next time. You can mentor them on how much easier and appropriate life is when you live by the rules at all times.

Court Rules on Civility and Lawyer Conduct

Court rules on civility abound. So do lawyer's oaths, most of which require the oath-taker to promise not to engage in incivility or unethical behavior. Check the federal and state courts in your jurisdiction to see whether those courts have separate rules pertaining to the conduct expected of lawyers practicing there. Discussing those rules with mentees will not only educate them about what courts expect, but will also cause your protégés to consider how important it is to know of such rules so that they are able to comply when they are in those courts.

American Inns of Court

You may already be a member of a chapter of the American Inns of Court, an organization dedicated to lawyer professionalism. If you aren't familiar with the organization, here is a description from its website, home.innsofcourt.org (under "What Is an American Inn of Court?"):

> The American Inns of Court is an association of lawyers, judges, and other legal professionals from all levels and backgrounds who share a passion for professional excellence. Through regular meetings, members are able to build and strengthen professional relationships; discuss fundamental concerns about professionalism and pressing legal issues of the day; share experiences and advice; exhort the utmost passion and dedication for the law; provide mentoring opportunities; and advance the highest levels of integrity, ethics, and civility.

You can see the emphasis it places on professionalism and on mentoring. If there is not a chapter near you but you are interested in joining, consider starting a chapter by contacting the national organization to find out how. That could be a wonderful project for you to work on with your mentee.

The Threat and Cost of Grievances

Finally, you owe it to your mentees to explain how lawyer misconduct is addressed, and how serious the consequences can be. You may invite your mentees to research some cases from your state's attorney discipline board, which are posted online, and then discuss them together. You may want to take your mentees to an attorney discipline hearing that is open to the public.

You will also want mentees to understand that certain convictions may result in automatic suspension of the license to practice law, and that they, and all attorneys—including the one representing the attorney in the criminal case—are required to report such convictions. Certainly, you will want them to understand the right of any client to file a grievance, and the obligation of every lawyer to report misconduct.

There are a variety of topics and information sources for mentoring on lawyer professionalism. We hope this chapter makes clear that *any* lawyer can engage as a professionalism mentor, even if you first must do a little research. And if research is necessary, we hope you will do that with your mentee.

CHAPTER 15

WHAT MENTEES BRING TO THE RELATIONSHIP
LIFELONG LEARNING

Imagine the Possibilities

Ponder what a protégé can bring to a mentor. If you keep an open mind about what you are receiving, along with what you are giving, you may learn much more than you expected. If lifelong learning is important to you, just imagine what you can learn from your protégé and you may be even more excited about mentoring!

AMY SAYS: I have always had a baby face, and even in my 60s, people still think I am much younger than I am. That can be a compliment but, frankly, it's always been a detriment in my work because others assume I am younger and less experienced than I am. I know from firsthand experience how annoying it is when people treat you as a neophyte and assume you have little experience or knowledge. Law was a third career for me.

Don't Assume (You Know What Happens When You Assume)

Start by not assuming anything about who you will be mentoring. Not everyone you mentor with will necessarily be in their 20s. New lawyers and law students may be in their 50s. They may have had successful careers in other fields. Don't judge their age and experience by the fact that they are in law school or just got their professional, or P, number. Law schools draw a significantly nontraditional crowd of students.

Also, you may be mentoring a lawyer who is new to your bar or firm but not new to practice. This lawyer may simply be new to the area and would like to learn about the local bench and bar.

This Isn't Just for the Old Guys

Some mentoring programs collect feedback from their participants, and they have found that millennial mentees sometimes say they would like to have a millennial mentor, or at least someone a little closer to their age. Protégés who are new attorneys may be more comfortable with someone closer to their age because they may understand each other better, share similar experiences, see the world the same way, or simply not want a more-established attorney to think they are stupid or green. So, be aware that mentoring programs can use mentors of all ages and experience levels. Less-experienced attorney mentors may benefit just as much from mentoring as the older attorneys, and they may start a lifelong commitment to mentoring.

Generational Characteristics

The everyday discussions about traits shared by generations really seems to have started in earnest when Generation X came along. Members of Gen X (born approximately 1965 to 1984) seemed so different that we sought out ways to understand them as a group. Researchers began exploring shared characteristics and found that political and social issues that occur during our childhoods can, indeed, contribute to shared characteristics and perspectives among people in the same age group.

AMY SAYS: I remember when my mother asked me how a fax machine worked, and that was the point in my life when I knew I could no longer understand or explain certain technologies. It's only gotten crazier since then. I recognize that there is a world out there that I am not a part of, but if you are a practicing attorney, you owe it to yourself to understand the world in which millennials have been raised.

While we won't delve into the various generational characteristics here, we must emphasize that the generational divide between baby boomers (born 1946-1964) and millennials is huge. Furthermore, it's likely that many boomers will be mentors nowadays, since they have reached the point in their careers when they have a lifetime of knowledge to share—and this while many mentees will be millennials, as most people in law school probably fall into that group. That leads to considerations when members of the two groups are paired.

Dive into the Great Divide

If you are a boomer mentoring a millennial, you might not believe that you can learn from them. Yes, some boomers are parents of millennials, and so you may have that perspective on them. But the more millennials you get to know, the better your understanding will be.

It's very likely that technology has created one of the greatest generational divides that has ever existed. Boomers didn't grow up with personal computers or the internet. They had to struggle to learn email in the '90s, not to mention just typing on a keyboard, along with getting a handle on Microsoft Word, spreadsheet software like Excel and, more recently, smartphones.

MATT SAYS: In my first 60-minute mentoring session as a law student, I was offered a clerkship in that attorney's office. Who would ever have dreamed! But he got to know me a little, I got to know him a little, I shared some technology insights I had about improving his office functions, and suddenly I had a job. The attorney was probably not thinking about that happening when he signed up to be a mentor, but he kept an open mind about me and saw an opportunity.

From being a latchkey kid to cyberbullying, from gaming to social networking, online dating, and having vast, borderless choices in music, books, movies, and TV shows, millennials have had a life experience unlike anything a boomer could have imagined at their age. And attorneys who are Gen Xers may have to admit that there are significant gaps between them and millennials, too.

So, imagine how much you can learn from a person who has had a completely different life experience from yours. Give that some serious thought before you determine that you should do all the talking when you mentor. Allow reverse mentoring to happen, and both parties will benefit.

A Potential Colleague or Firm Partner

As you mentor a new attorney or law student, recognize that you may be meeting your future partner, associate, clerk, colleague, or adversary in practice. Keep that in mind when you think of the impression you may be leaving. But keep that in mind, also, for opportunities that may arise for you, your business or firm, or someone you know who may be looking for someone just like your protégé. This is not to suggest that the protégé should be using mentoring to job hunt. But you have an opportunity to observe someone when he or she is not in interviewing mode, and you might like what you see.

Of course, if the mentee is settled into a job already, you may still cross paths in any number of professional circumstances. Keep your mind open to the range of potential interactions, and remember that it is as important for you to make a good impression as it is for the mentee.

Is This the Beginning of a Beautiful Relationship?

Matt's experience of being offered a job after a one-hour mentoring session is not typical, but it changed everything for him. Not only did he need the income to support his family, he was suddenly very excited about the opportunities presented by episodic mentoring. His mentoring attorney became Matt's temporary employer, and also a confidant and colleague. This led Matt to want to have many more mentoring episodes to build his network of attorney acquaintances and continue learning.

The same can be said for mentors. Imagine the people you'll meet through episodic mentoring! You will get outside your normal sphere of relationships and create new relationships and, who knows? Maybe even make new friends.

By promoting one-hour mentoring, we are not in any way attempting to say it's better than having a matched, long-term mentor. However, we believe that a long-term mentoring relationship should be one that springs from trust—*not* one that springs from a blind match. By engaging in 60-minute mentoring, hopefully a few or more times, two people have a chance to figure out if they click, understand each other, get along, and want to meet again. What better foundation could there be from which to explore a possible long-term mentoring relationship?

PART 4

FOR BAR
ASSOCIATIONS

CHAPTER 16

EPISODIC MENTORING FOR MEMBERSHIP DEVELOPMENT
10-MINUTE MENTORING INVITATIONAL

Recruiting New Bar Association Members

Local bar associations are generally focused on recruiting, and some have various types of recruiting events. We found success, and had a lot of fun, using 10-minute mentoring during recruiting events for our Inn of Court chapter. Because the American Inns of Court are devoted to professionalism and encourage mentoring, we decided it was a natural fit to demonstrate some brief mentoring during these recruiting events. It gave interested attorneys a chance to talk with a number of the chapter's members one on one, as well as a chance to see that mentoring is important to our group. And it proved to be interesting and entertaining.

If your bar wants to offer episodic mentoring as a regular benefit of membership, this would be a good way to feature it and recruit at the same time.

Our Inn of Court Event Program

We used 10-minute mentoring increments, encouraged reverse mentoring, and dedicated an hour to the whole process so that each potential member had a chance to sit with at least six attorneys. Here we share information from a handout used in past programs as an example to inspire your bar association to consider a similar recruiting event.

10-MINUTE MENTORING INVITATIONAL: PROGRAM

5:30 – 6:30 p.m.

10-Minute Mentoring

Help yourself to cocktails and hors d'oeuvres while you engage in 10-minute mentoring. Guests, please approach someone with a different color name tag and an M. Mentor each other for 10 minutes (5 minutes each).

Every 10 minutes, a whistle will blow and each guest must find a new partner and repeat the process. Sample questions are provided on the back of this program.

6:30 – 6:45 p.m.

Welcome from the President of the Thomas M. Cooley Inn of Court

Please refill your drinks and plates and have a seat.

6:45 – 7:30 p.m.

Stories from mid-Michigan Lawyers: Learning from Unexpected Sources

[Attorney 1 / Attorney 2 / Attorney 3]

7:20 – 7:30 p.m.

Mingle and please take a membership packet with you.

See mentoring guidelines.

10-MINUTE MENTORING GUIDELINES

Mentoring can occur between any two people regardless of age, experience, and outlook. Old can learn from young; experienced can learn from non-experienced.

Members and guests have name tags in three different colors (and Inn members have an M on their tag). The colors represent the number of years the attorney has been a member of the bar. Pair up with someone who has a different color name tag, and guests, please choose members.

Each of you has 5 minutes to mentor the other. If you cannot think of anything you can offer the other person, here are some questions you can ask each other that will help you elicit information that could benefit you in your professional development:

- Is there something or someone who made an impact on your professional development and what was that impact? Why was it good or bad?

- Describe an ethical challenge you have faced and how you dealt with it.

- Tell me about an important lesson you learned about being responsible.

- What good came from your worst experience?

- How can I best avoid getting into ethical trouble in my role as an attorney?

- What is your life philosophy?

- What is the best input you could give me about understanding someone like you?

- What can you share with me from your experience that you think would help me in my work as a professional?

Of course, this can be adjusted to 15- or 20-minute mentoring increments, and the questions can be changed to accommodate whatever goal you have in mind.

Note that **we used reverse mentoring—so that each person mentored the other**—and provided questions that could be asked and answered by either party. They were free, however, to mentor each other in any way they wanted. We also gave them enough questions that they could pick and choose the one or two they had time to discuss.

Why Mentoring Works as a Recruiting Tool

Mentoring during a recruiting event can showcase the emphasis that an association puts on mentoring, which is something new members are looking for. Plus, it's a great way to make sure everyone circulates. It creates a sense of ease and excitement, while also signaling to current members about the importance of mentoring.

What Mentees Want

If you are a board member of or an administrator for a bar association that is trying to build its membership, it's important to remember what new members want from their affiliation with you. Most of what they are looking for falls into the category of mentoring. They typically want to:

- Meet and network with other bar members.
- Keep up on new developments in the law.
- Attend social events with people who understand what their professional life is about.
- Find role models.
- Contribute to service and other giving programs of the association.
- Develop professional relationships with attorneys and judges whom they may encounter in their future work.

Keep in mind that millennials, in particular, are accustomed to having many mentors. Start with their mom, dad, possibly a step-parent or two, and the slew of grandparents who come with that package. And they have a thousand friends on Facebook and Instagram. Millennials grew up seeking advice from all these sources and more, so the idea of having just one mentor as a professional guide may seem ridiculous to them. Millennials are fond of saying that they're not looking for one mentor—they're looking for a Board of Directors.

This section explains how all those goals can be accomplished through episodic mentoring. But suffice it to say for now that a recruiting event dedicated to mentoring and making sure the guests have meaningful, though short, conversations with as many members as possible, tells the future member/mentee that this association offers what the mentee is seeking. In other words, recruiting without offering mentoring, or with offering only one mentor, may not be as successful in attracting today's newest attorneys.

CHAPTER 17

EPISODIC MENTORING FOR NEW MEMBERS
WELCOMING, ASSIMILATING, SUPPORTING

Welcoming

There may be no better way to welcome new bar members than to immediately offer them a number of mentors, whose role will be to help them learn and adopt the shared values of the association. This can be done through episodic mentoring, where the new members are encouraged to spend an hour apiece with a number of established members over their first year of membership.

With such an intentional program, you can be assured that the new member will have quality time with existing members—at least an hour—without overburdening any one member to mentor that person for a year. And group mentoring may play a key role here, where new members can meet with three or four current members in a lunchtime mentoring session dedicated to discussing the association's goals.

Assimilating and Enculturating

Your bar association may want to consider offering a one-year episodic mentoring program to not only welcome new members, but to help them assimilate the established culture of your association. This is especially important for affinity bar associations that exist for that very purpose.

Episodic mentoring is uniquely helpful for enculturating new members because it involves the new member meeting for only one hour with many current members—

meaning the new member will be exposed to the viewpoints and values that various members have about the purpose of the association.

Mentoring New Members for Success

It goes without saying that some of the most critical mentoring that can occur in the first stages of a new attorney's career is in the subject matter, skills, practices, and procedures with which that new attorney will be working. Subject matter or practice area mentoring may already be happening in your bar association because it is the most common type of mentoring offered.

You obviously want the members of your bar to succeed, so if you don't already offer practice area mentoring, you really should. As part of your first-year episodic mentoring program, consider offering guidance to new members in these areas:

- New lawyer advertising and other methods of marketing
- Law office management, billing, and retainer procedures
- Client intake/interviews
- Client management
- Business development
- Taking court-appointed cases (walk-through of typical felony appointment from the clerk's call or email through trial in circuit court)
- Preparations for pretrial and preliminary hearings, case evaluation, mediation, arbitration, and trial
- Holding preliminary exams
- Jury selection tactics
- Sentencing guidelines
- Objecting to and taking depositions
- Drafting, arguing, and filing motions
- Local court rules
- Settling cases

You could ask bar members to select a topic from this list and discuss it when they have their one-hour mentoring episode with the new member. It will be much more productive than spending an hour just getting to know each other, although that can certainly constitute the first 15 minutes.

A Way to Steer Clear of Overburdening Members

Episodic mentoring is especially helpful in mentoring new members because a single mentor can never sufficiently cover all pertinent subject matter and procedural questions without spending an inordinate amount of time on mentoring. To employ episodic mentoring so as not to overburden your members, throw the just-discussed list out to them and ask them to pick one topic on which they can mentor the new attorney for an hour. If more than one mentor discusses the same topic, this will also benefit the mentee who will be learning different perspectives on the topic.

Different members will also have different relationships with local judges and lawyers, and the mentees will benefit from learning which members may be helpful in introducing them to the local bench and bar.

How to Administer an Episodic Mentoring Program

There is matching involved in episodic mentoring, but only by available time. The program administrator can keep a shared calendar and ask all members who are interested in mentoring to sign up for a one-hour slot (or as many one-hour slots as they may like to have) for each quarter of the year.

You can offer these one-hour slots on a named or a blind basis (blind meaning the attorney's name won't be listed). If you have a few very popular mentors with whom all the protégés want to meet, you may want to offer their time slots on a blind basis. That may also send a message that every volunteer mentor is considered valuable and has good things to offer.

On the other hand, to make sure protégés get one hour with all volunteer mentors, you may eventually have to name them. Or, the administrator can keep track of who has met with whom and make sure there is a different match each time.

Then mentees can access the calendar and take the one-hour appointments that fit their schedule. That is probably the simplest way to create mentoring episodes in your bar organization. But you may find other approaches that work better as the program continues.

The program administrator may also want to send a standard email to protégés confirming the mentoring episode and informing them with whom they will be mentoring and where. That email should include any additional information that might be helpful, as well as a reminder to dress professionally and be on time.

The Payoff

Think how great it will be for new association members to spend an hour with multiple current members during their first year of membership. They will expand or create their own network, feel a part of the organization, and be more confident about their first steps in practice. In addition, they will meet lawyers they bond with and feel they can go to for help, and likely be eager to help mentor the next set of new members.

CHAPTER 18

EPISODIC MENTORING FOR ATTORNEY DEVELOPMENT
GROUP MENTORING AMONG MEMBERS

Continuing Legal Education

Your members will, of course, have access to continuing legal education resources offered by your state, and in most states, they will be required to participate in a minimum number of CLE hours. Consider offering a "group mentoring" version of that through your bar association. Here is how it might be set up.

Spread the Love

Attorneys will be attending different CLE sessions during the year. Ask them to report back what they learned to interested members. This will constitute a form of group mentoring, with the attorney who attended the CLE program acting as the mentor in teaching the group

Likewise, you could ask members who attend professional conferences to offer one-hour sessions on information they picked up that could be helpful to others.

Your Internal Experts

Next, consider this: As your attorney members continue to handle complex cases, as they spend years handling the same types of matters, they are becoming subject-matter experts. If they had time, they would probably write a book on their area of expertise. Episodic mentoring can offer them a way to summarize their knowledge in particular areas and teach it to group members (without having to invest the considerable time needed to write a book).

If you are a county or affinity bar association and not one based in a common practice area, you may be surprised how **many of your members would take an hour to listen to a presentation by another member on a topic unrelated to their practice area.** Attorneys join bar associations for camaraderie and friendship, but they also have a desire to continue to learn about other areas of the law and especially newer, burgeoning areas of practice. They may just be curious about those areas, or they may see a connection between that subject and what they currently do. Or they may see a new niche area developing that they could add to their practice.

While this may seem more like presenting than mentoring, the theme of episodic mentoring is simple—anytime you are teaching or guiding, you are mentoring. So consider such presentations group mentoring, but be sure to keep their format to an hour. Everyone will appreciate that.

CHAPTER 19

PARTNERING WITH A LOCAL LAW SCHOOL
STUDENT AND REVERSE MENTORING OPPORTUNITIES

Note: You may not have a law school in your area, but you will want to read this chapter anyway, as you may be inspired to see opportunities with a law school even hundreds of miles away.

Growing Membership by Offering to Mentor Students

Bar associations spend a great deal of time recruiting new members. Establishing a pipeline from the local law school to the bar association can help achieve the recruiting goal. The best way for a bar association to reach those soon-to-be graduates is through 60-minute mentoring that pairs lawyer members of the association with law students seeking mentoring episodes.

Clearly, the local bar has a vested interest in mentoring law students who could become members. Those who get to know some of the attorneys through mentoring will be more likely to become members themselves. And when they do become members, having existing relationships in the association will help them assimilate more quickly. Also, both parties will benefit from the new attorney understanding the importance of professionalism, having already been mentored on that topic while in law school.

If your local law school has not considered episodic professionalism mentoring, the bar association is perfectly positioned to suggest it to the school and to offer one-hour time slots with members.

Mentoring for Service to the Community

There can probably be no finer mentoring of law students than that which occurs when the student assists an attorney with a pro bono case. Such mentoring may not exactly fit the one-hour model, but it will fit the concept of mentoring in episodes.

Work with your local law school to set up a pro bono mentoring program that matches students with attorneys who want to take on a pro bono case occasionally. The student should do as much of the legal work as possible—under the attorney's supervision and within the limits of the ethics rules, of course.

This pro bono mentoring will not only help the student get legal experience, it will encourage your lawyer members to engage in more pro bono service than they otherwise might, as they will be primarily supervising and have less of the actual case work to do. Of course, supervision involves teaching and guiding (mentoring), and perhaps editing, and that may be a nice change of pace for the lawyers.

Participating students will also get to experience firsthand the excitement and grati-fication that comes from using a law degree to help those who otherwise might lack access to justice.

More important, the mentoring you provide through the program will send the important message that pro bono service is an obligation of all attorneys. When law students see that attorneys not only find time to take cases pro bono, but are also committed to the concept of giving back, it is the best type of role-modeling.

Orientation Professionalism Mentoring

If your local law school doesn't already offer an orientation session on professional-ism, offer to provide mentors from your membership for one. A typical orientation program on professionalism requires a two-hour commitment from bar members. During that time, they will introduce themselves to the incoming class and then part-ner with another attorney to lead small group discussions about ethics and profes-sionalism with the incoming students.

It's a great way for new law students to learn firsthand the importance of ethics and professionalism in the practice of law, along with the emphasis that practicing lawyers place on professionalism. They also get to meet "real" attorneys, and may become interested in mentoring with those attorneys when they are ready to engage in epi-sodic mentoring.

Turning the Tables: Quid Pro Quo

One of the less obvious benefits and most exciting developments from Cooley Law School's episodic mentoring program with the local bar was this realization: that we—the law school—could mentor the attorneys in that bar.

In fact, this chapter was inspired by a brainstorming session Amy had with board members of the local county bar association. She approached them to ask if they would allow her to recruit their members for 60-minute mentoring sessions with her students. But she felt she should not come calling without bringing gifts from her school. So she asked the bar board members what the law school might do for them in return for their members helping mentor law students.

They came up with four distinct areas where law faculty could mentor their members. Amy considered that reverse mentoring, but they did not—they fondly thought of their former law teachers as lifelong mentors.

Niche and Practice Area Mentoring

Our local bar wanted mentoring for its members—many of them graduates of our school—in topics that might help them discover possible practice areas, or grow the area of practice they had decided to pursue. And we were anxious to offer what we knew about both standard and developing areas of law. We relied primarily on our adjunct faculty and LL.M. faculty who had recent if not ongoing practices of their own and had developed a broader understanding of those areas through their teaching.

For example, participating adjunct faculty were practitioners who had both a practice and an academic background in their areas of expertise. So an adjunct who taught, for example, disability law, knew the latest federal and state cases because he or she taught those very cases at the school, and also practiced in that area for a living. We asked the adjunct faculty members to offer one- to four-hour group mentoring (training) sessions to local bar members who were either new and looking for a practice area, or who were interested in expanding their practice to a new or related area.

We also identified evolving niche practice areas that new attorneys could be exposed to and further develop if they had an interest. Topics included emerging issues in areas like insurance law, while other areas were those in which members of the Young Lawyers Section could develop a niche practice, such as foreclosure, bankruptcy, the Servicemembers Civil Relief Act, information technology law, and trademark and copyright.

For example, our school offers an LL.M. in insurance law, and is located in one of the country's most heavily populated locations for insurance company national headquarters. So we asked our LL.M. faculty to offer a three-hour mentoring session covering the basics of insurance law. Lawyers who attended were extraordinarily appreciative of what they learned in that brief session, and indicated it was enough to help them decide about insurance law as a potential practice area. They were now in a better position to interview with some of the companies, as they had a broad understanding of the legal issues involved in insurance.

In addition, the faculty members who taught agreed to mentor attorneys who wanted mentoring in that subject area as their practice developed.

New Lawyer Mentoring

The school's adjunct faculty also agreed to help with the new lawyer mentoring explained in the previous chapter. The Young Lawyers Section recruited adjunct faculty and local judges who were willing to spend a Saturday mentoring new lawyers on anything from how to behave in their courtrooms, to how to take a case from client interview to verdict or judgment in the local court system. Faculty joined with the local judges and experienced bar association members to teach new lawyers basic practice skills that may not have been covered in their law school coursework.

Full-day new lawyer mentoring sessions can be offered twice a year at the law school or bar following release of bar exam results and swearing-in ceremonies. That is a very reassuring way to welcome new lawyers into the profession and provides a wonderful opportunity for them to meet their new colleagues.

An especially nice outcome of our school's new lawyer mentoring was that the members of the bench expressed their appreciation for knowing who the new attorneys were, so that they wouldn't meet them for the first time in a case they were hearing.

Ongoing Attorney Development

The previous chapter covered mentoring for attorney development and continuing legal education, and that type of mentoring can also be done in collaboration with the law school. Your bar group simply asks the local law school to invite their faculty to be presenters on new and developing legal trends. For example, two of our constitutional law professors presented annually on decisions issued during the year by the U.S. Supreme Court and the implications for practice. It was one of the most well-attended of the local bar's luncheon lecture series.

Training Lawyers for Pro Bono Service

Bar associations can also encourage the local law school to provide training to members in areas of law that will help and encourage them to provide pro bono service—and work with a law student on the case. For example, at Cooley Law School, we provided training for lawyers statewide in the Servicemembers Civil Relief Act. This was part of our effort to get lawyers to take pro bono cases of service members returning from deployment and confronting legal issues. Along with wanting to help those service members, we wanted our students to get legal experience through pro bono work.

By bringing in experts who could provide this type of training to lawyers for free, we were able to accomplish both goals: Lawyers came because they wanted the free training, and all we asked in return was that they take one pro bono case and work on it with a law student.

Making It Happen

If your local law school has not initiated any of these types of collaborative efforts, it's incumbent on the local bar association to take the lead and incentivize that collaboration. The bar gains new members and provides current members with training and education, while the law school gains episodic mentors for its students and a chance to help them develop the needed values, and perhaps career leads. The community wins because more lawyers and law students are providing pro bono and public service. So reach out to the school, give them a copy of this book, and mark this chapter for them.

QUICK REFERENCES

Characteristics that will help you become a successful professional that can be taught or modeled by a mentor

- Personal ethics including honesty and candor
- Dedication to thorough research and excellent work product
- Civility
- Inquisitiveness
- Patience
- Open-mindedness
- Dependability
- Preparation
- Cultural competency (how to understand others)
- Enjoying people
- Integrity (doing the right thing when no one and everyone is watching)

Skills required of you as a lawyer that can be taught or modeled by a mentor

- Problem-solving
- Legal analysis and reasoning
- Legal research
- Factual investigation
- Communication
- Counseling
- Negotiation
- Alternative dispute resolution
- Litigation
- Organization and management of legal work
- Recognizing and resolving ethical dilemmas
- Dealing with difficult people
- Handling a budget
- Running a meeting

- Inspiring others to be their best
- Strategic planning
- Managing people, including focusing their work on a strategic plan
- Setting fees and billing clients
- Marketing and business development

Proactive self-mentoring techniques

- Information seeking ("How do you know when to ... ?")
- Feedback seeking ("I am thinking about externing in the Attorney General's Office. What are your thoughts on that?")
- Relationship-building ("I read about your pending case in the newspaper and would love to sit in on your upcoming trial." "I see you are a graduate of Cooley Law School and I would like to hear about how Cooley prepared you for your practice.")
- General socializing ("How do you like being a member of this bar section?")
- Positive framing/reputation ("I have looked forward to meeting you because of your success in starting the professionalism orientation program at Michigan law schools.")
- Learning "language and customs" ("Your clerk was kind enough to explain to me when motion day is and how I can observe a trial in your courtroom.")

Questions you can ask virtually anyone for self-mentoring

- What do you like best about your job? What don't you like?
- What does your best day at work involve? Your worst?
- How do you deal with difficult people?
- What is the most challenging thing you have faced professionally?
- Have you ever encountered an ethical challenge and how did you deal with it?
- How do you keep your skills up?
- What advice would you give someone who is just starting out?
- How did you get your first job?
- How do you balance your personal life and work life?
- How do you stay healthy?

Matt's go-to questions to ask attorneys

- Why do you like this type of law?
- How did you choose to practice this type of law?
- What is your least favorite part of (area of law, having your own business, working here.)?
- What is your favorite part?
- What is the best thing I should do now to prepare myself to practice?
- What was the best thing that ever happened to you as a lawyer?
- What are your thoughts on mediation?
- Are moot court or mock trial important to see on a résumé of a young attorney?
- What is something that you like to see on a new graduate's résumé?
- What is the most important thing you look for in hiring a young attorney?
- What is the best career move you have ever made? Worst?
- How did you find a mentor when you needed one?
- How active is the local bar?

How a mentor can help a protégé

- Help you with specific concerns about law school or lawyering
- Expose you to the legal world through shadowing and discussion
- Supervise you in their pro bono work or join you for public service work
- Discuss legal issues you need help with and share knowledge about areas of law
- Expose you to and educate you about a specific practice area
- Describe how they balance work and personal life
- Share professional experiences and insights that will help you grow
- Be a role model for appropriate and professional behavior
- Help you grow professionally by teaching you what they know about professional conduct and development
- Talk with you about your own professional development plan
- Review your professionalism portfolio
- Introduce you to people who employ their law degrees in ways that interest you and help you develop a network of attorney contacts
- Teach you about ethical challenges and how to handle them
- Review your résumé and cover letter
- Conduct a mock interview with you

- Introduce you to people who are looking for externs or employees
- Write a letter of recommendation
- Give advice on how to make a successful transition from law student to bar examinee to attorney, including both the good moves and the mistakes the mentor made in the process
- Attend professional events together, such as bar association meetings
- Allow you to do some legal research or writing

Resources for law students to connect with attorneys

- Law school alumni office.
- State bar associations, for both the state in which you are located while in law school and the state in which you intend to practice law.
- Local and affinity bar associations. Most counties in the state in which you are located have a local bar association. You may also find such associations by metropolitan area, such as the New York City Bar Association, and by interest and affinity, for example, the Criminal Defense Attorneys of Michigan and the Armenian-American or B'Nai B'rith Barristers Bar Association). Most of these associations welcome student members and offer membership for free or low cost.
- American Inns of Court. See if a chapter is located in your vicinity and how you can attend as a guest or even join as a law student or young lawyer.
- Legal fraternities. Your law school student bar association may have student chapters of such legal fraternities and honor societies such as Phi Delta Phi and Phi Alpha Delta—both devoted to professionalism, ethics, and service. These fraternities boast many graduates who are now practicing law or using their JDs in their work. Joining a student fraternity may open the door to meeting the alumni of these fraternities.
- The courtroom. This is a fertile place to meet attorneys. There you will find lawyers and judges who, at the end of the day, may be interested in who you are and why you've been sitting in the courtroom. If you are hoping to meet lawyers this way, be sure you are wearing a suit when you sit in on a trial or on motion day.
- Lawyer directories. The advanced search on Martindale.com, for example, allows you to search by law school, practice area, locality, and other relevant factors.
- Law school faculty. They are all lawyers and may have much to offer you in your professional development.

RESOURCES

Eileen S. Johnson, Amy Timmer, Dawn E. Chandler, & Charles R. Toy, "Matched vs. Episodic Mentoring: An Exploration of the Processes and Outcomes for Law School Students Engaged in Professional Mentoring," Vol. 23, No. 1, *Legal Education Review* (Fall 2013).

Ida Abbott, *The Lawyer's Guide to Mentoring,* Second Edition (NALP 2018).

Civility Matters (American Board of Trial Advocates, 2011).

Lang, Hon. Douglas S., "Cultivating Honesty, Integrity, and Civility: The Essence of Professionalism," *For the Defense,* June, 2010, p. 68.

Weresh, Melissa H., "I'll Start Walking Your Way, You Start Walking Mine: Sociological Perspectives on Professional Identity Development and Influence of Generational Differences," *South Carolina Law Review.* Winter, 2009. 61 S.C. L. Rev. 337.

Hamilton, Neil and Brabbit, Lisa Montpetit, "Fostering Professionalism Through Mentoring," *Journal of Legal Education,* Volume 57, Number 1 (March 2007).

"Transition Into Law Practice Program Pilot Project," Committee on the Standards of the Profession, State Bar of Georgia, January 1, 2000 – December 31, 2001.

National Legal Mentoring Consortium, www.legalmentoring.org

Attorney at Work Bookstore, www.attorneyatwork.com

If you want to be a mentor and don't know any protégés who would appreciate your guidance, contact me at WMU Cooley Law School. I'll find a mentee for you who will really appreciate your time. — Amy Timmer

ONE REALLY GOOD IDEA EVERY DAY

attorney at work @

Attorney at Work publishes the website
AttorneyatWork.com, providing lawyers with
practice tips and advice on building successful
and satisfying law practices, in addition to guides
and books for the legal profession. To subscribe
to free daily and weekly newsletters,
visit **www.attorneyatwork.com.**